westermann

W0319158

NOTTING HILL GATE

Workbook 5

Erarbeitet von:
Theresa Künzel-Giller (Pforzheim), Gabriele Linke (Marburg), Cedric Lütgert (Marburg), Sascha Mohr (Wiesbaden), Maike Pegler (Sarstedt/Gödringen), Sabina Piatzer (Hannover), Dr. Ivo Steininger (Wetzlar)

Fachliche Beratung:
Angela Berkenkamp (Wetzlar), Susanne Quandt (Bremen)

Notting Hill Gate 5
Workbook

Zusatzmaterialien zu Notting Hill Gate 5

Für Lehrkräfte:
- Textbook für Lehrkräfte 5 (ISBN 978-3-14-128284-9)
- Materialien für Lehrkräfte 5 (ISBN 978-3-14-128294-8)
- Lernerfolgskontrollen 5 (ISBN 978-3-14-128320-4)
- CD für Lehrkräfte 5 (ISBN 978-3-14-128304-4)
- DVD für Lehrkräfte 5 (ISBN 978-3-14-128314-3)
- Online-Diagnose zu Notting Hill Gate 5
  www.onlinediagnose.de

Für Schülerinnen und Schüler:
- Textbook 5 (ISBN 978-3-14-128200-9)
- Interaktive Übungen 5 (WEB-14-128220)
- Arbeitsbuch Inklusion 5 (inkl. Audios)
  (ISBN 978-3-14-128230-6)
- Klassenarbeitstrainer 5 (ISBN 978-3-14-128246-7)
- Grammatiktrainer 5 (ISBN 978-3-14-128386-0)
- Wortschatztrainer 5 (ISBN 978-3-14-128240-5)
- Westermann Vokabeltrainer-App zu Notting Hill Gate 5
  www.westermann.de/vokabeltrainer

Das digitale Schulbuch und digitale Unterrichtsmaterialien für Schülerinnen und Schüler und für Lehrkräfte finden Sie in der BiBox – dem digitalen Unterrichtssystem passend zum Lehrwerk. Mehr Informationen über aktuelle Lizenzen finden Sie auf www.bibox.schule.

www.westermann.de/nhg

Über diesen QR-Code gelangst du auf die Webseite
www.westermann.de/128210
Dort findest du alle Audiotracks, Videoclips, Arbeitsblätter zur Medienbildung und die Practise more Arbeitsblätter.

westermann GRUPPE

Druck A[1] / Jahr 2022
Alle Drucke der Serie A sind im Unterricht parallel verwendbar.

Redaktion: Jutta Eckardt-Scheurig
Illustrationen: Mario Ellert, Bremen
Umschlaggestaltung: LIO Design GmbH, Braunschweig
Layout: LIO Design GmbH, Braunschweig
Druck und Bindung: Westermann Druck GmbH, Georg-Westermann-Allee 66, 38104 Braunschweig

ISBN 978-3-14-**128210**-8

Inhaltsverzeichnis

In diesem Workbook findest du folgende Verweise und Arten von Aufgaben:

1 audio	Zu dieser Aufgabe gibt es einen Audiotrack.
2 video	Zu dieser Aufgabe gibt es einen Videoclip.
3 wordbank	In den Wordbanks im Textbook sind die Wörter nach Wortfeldern geordnet.
4 skill	Auf den Skills-Seiten im Textbook findest du Tipps und Strategien fürs Lernen.
5 grammar	Zu dieser Aufgabe gibt es Erklärungen im Grammatik-Teil des Textbooks.
6	Dieses Symbol kennzeichnet Aufgaben, in denen du Medienkompetenz aufbaust und trainierst. Zu diesen Aufgaben gibt es Arbeitsblätter auf der Webseite.
7 CHOOSE YOUR LEVEL	Bei diesen Aufgaben gibt es drei unterschiedliche Schwierigkeitsgrade: **leicht** **mittel** **schwierig**
8 CHOOSE YOUR TASK	Hier gibt es drei Aufgaben, von denen du dir eine aussuchen kannst. Du kannst alleine, mit einem Partner oder einer Partnerin oder in einer Gruppe arbeiten.
DIGITAL+	Dieser Hinweis zeigt, dass es zusätzliches Material auf der Webseite gibt.
Practise reading	Hier erhältst du praktische Tipps, um deine Lesekompetenz zu schulen.
Challenge	So werden schwierige Zusatzaufgaben gekennzeichnet.
TARGET TASK SUPPORT	Hier findest du Hilfen zu den Target Tasks (Zielaufgaben) im Textbook.

What's in the street?

1a audio 1/1

Listen and number the things in the picture.

1b

Look at the picture. Tick ✓ yes or no.

Can you see …

	yes	no
1 … a tree?		
2 … a green house?		
3 … an old lady?		
4 … a pink car?		
5 … a mobile phone?		

1c

Complete the sentences.

1 I can see a red __________

2 I can see a blue __________

3 I can see a black __________

4 I can see a yellow __________

5 I can see a green __________

6 I can see a purple __________

1d

Sort the words into the lists.

~~apples~~ · dog · house · carrots · cat · girl · bike · boy · car · child · bus stop · park

food	animals	people	other words
apples			

1e

Look at the picture. Find more words for the lists.

Ice cream flavours

2a

Label the ice cream flavours.

mango ______

______

______

______

______

______

______

______

2b audio 1/3

Which ice cream flavours do the children like? Listen and tick ✓.

1

☐ vanilla
☐ chocolate
☐ strawberry

2

☐ mango
☐ cherry
☐ banana

3

☐ orange
☐ lemon
☐ kiwi

2c audio 1/2

Listen to the ice cream chant and number the pictures.

☐ 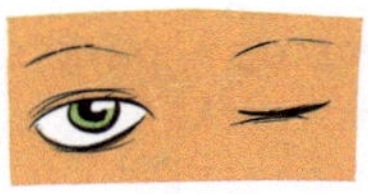 → ☐  → ☐ 

☐  → ☐  → 1 

At the ice cream van

3a audio 1/5

Listen and complete the speech bubbles. Use the words from the box.

places · welcome · skateboard · please

1 That's a nice ______________________ .

2 I don't know any good ______________________ in Notting Hill.

3 ______________________ to Notting Hill then.

4 Next, ______________________ !

3b

Match the children and the speech bubbles. Draw lines.

Sorry, just a minute.

That's a nice skateboard.

I'm new around here.

Welcome to Notting Hill then.

Harry meets Ava

4a

Read TB4a again. Answer the questions.

Ava · Harry · Joshua · Lily · Noah · Tarek

1 Who has got a twin sister? ______________________

2 Who has got two brothers? ______________________

3 Who is six? ______________________

4 Who is Ava's friend? ______________________

5 Who is twelve? ______________________

6 Who is eleven? ______________________

4b

Match the questions and the answers. Draw lines.

1 Do you skateboard?	I'm Harry.
2 Where do you go skateboarding?	Sure. It's 07984631205.
3 Where are you from?	Yes, I do.
4 What's your name?	I'm eleven.
5 How old are you?	In the park.
6 Can I have your phone number?	I'm from Brighton.

4c audio 1/7

Listen to the children. Write down the phone numbers.

1 My phone number is ______________________

2 My phone number is ______________________

3 My phone number is ______________________

4 My phone number is ______________________

The next day

5a

Write down the children's names.

1 ______________________

2 ______________________

3 ______________________

4 ______________________

5 ______________________

5b

Read the dialogue in TB5a again. Complete the sentences.

1 Hi Ava. This is my ______________ Lily.

2 Hi Harry, hi Lily. This is Tarek. And that's my ______________ Noah.

3 Hi. Nice to ______________ you.

4 Are you from ______________________________, too?

5 Yes, I am. How ______________ are you?

6 We're twins. We're ______________. And you?

7 I'm ______________.

8 I'm twelve, too. Come on, let's ______________.

5c

Look at the picture and answer the questions.

1 Who has got a blue helmet? ______________________________

2 Who has got a grey helmet? ______________________________

3 Who has got green shoes? ______________________________

4 Who has got a red jacket? ______________________________

5 Who has got a yellow skateboard? ______________________________

Hi, what's your name?

6a

Put the dialogue in the right order.

1 Hi, what's your name?

3 Where are you from?

5 How old are you?

7 Have you got brothers and sisters?

9 What's your sister's name?

11 How old is she?

☐ I'm eleven.

☐ She's twelve.

☐ Her name is Rosalie.

2 Hi, my name is Jake.

☐ I've got one sister.

☐ I'm from London.

6b

Complete the sentences.

two brothers · very good · ten · black and white · name · name · six and eight

1 My ______ is Fatma. 2 I've got a sister and ______ .

3 My sister is ______ .

4 My brothers are ______ years old.

5 I like skateboarding. I'm ______ at it.

6 We've got a cat. Her ______ is Bubu. 7 She is ______ and very sweet.

Ava's little brother

7

What do you know about Ava's little brother? Write down Joshua's answers. Check with TB4a.

1 What's your name? *My name is Joshua.*

2 Where are you from? ______

3 How old are you? ______

4 Have you got brothers and sisters? ______

5 What's your favourite ice cream? ______

Die Check out-Seiten helfen dir einzuschätzen, was du schon gut kannst. Löse die Aufgaben auf dieser Doppelseite und male jeweils den ersten Kreis wie bei einer Ampel rot, gelb oder grün aus. Der zweite Kreis ist für die Lehrkraft.

Rot: Das kann ich noch nicht.

Gelb: Das fällt mir noch schwer.

Grün: Das kann ich gut.

1 Kannst du jemanden begrüßen und dich verabschieden?
2 Kannst du jemandem Fragen stellen?
3 Kannst du dich vorstellen?
4 Kannst du jemand anderen vorstellen?
5 Kannst du Telefonnummern verstehen und mitteilen?

1

Sort the sentences.

Bye. · Hi. · Nice to meet you. · Goodbye. · See you tomorrow. · Hello. · Good morning.

You come and say:	**You go and say:**

Ich kann jemanden begrüßen und mich verabschieden. ◯ ◯

2

You meet this boy. What can you ask him? Unscramble the questions.

1 name? - your - What's ______

2 are - How old – you? ______

3 from? - are you - Where ______

4 ice cream flavour? - the best - What's

______

5 your phone number? - have - Can I

______

Ich kann jemandem Fragen stellen. ◯ ◯

3

Write about yourself.

1 What's your name? ______

2 Where are you from? ______

3 How old are you? ______

4 Have you got a brother or a sister? ______

5 What's your phone number? ______

Ich kann mich vorstellen.

4

What can Mia and Leo say? Write it down.

Bill, Mia's friend | Mia | Hanah, Mia's sister | Alice, Leo's friend | Leo | Frank, Leo's brother

Mia: *This* ______ *and that* ______

Leo: ______

Ich kann jemand anderen vorstellen.

5a audio 1/9

Listen and write down the children's phone numbers.

1 Minnie's phone number: ______

2 Jacob's phone number: ______

5b

Say these phone numbers. Record yourself.

1 01545087908

2 01658801795

3 01965032804

Ich kann Telefonnummern verstehen und mitteilen.

In Ava's room

1a
wordbank: at home p. 158

What can you see? Write words in the picture.

1b

Look at the picture again. Write sentences.

You can write:

There is ______________________

There is a green ______________________

____

____

____

____

____

There are ______________________

There are three ______________________

____

____

____

____

1c

Read about Ava in TB1b again. Sort the words.

~~blue~~ · mum · always hungry · playing computer games · dad · skateboarding · four · two brothers · small garden · Notting Hill · carrots

her house	*her hobbies*	*her family*	*Ollie*
blue			

Challenge: **Add more words from the text.**

Ava

2a CHOOSE YOUR LEVEL audio 1/11

Listen to Ava.

I Tick ✓ the words you hear.

☐ room → ☐ garden → ☐ sofa

☐ hamster → ☐ name → ☐ friends

☐ brothers → ☐ laptop → ☐ skateboarding

II Are the sentences true or false? Tick ✓.

		true	false
1	Our house is small.	☐	☐
2	I've got a sofa.	☐	☐
3	My bed is grey.	☐	☐
4	The lion's name is Sammy.	☐	☐
5	I drink orange juice.	☐	☐

III Tick ✓ the correct sentence endings.

1	Ava's room is	☐ big.	☐ nice.	☐ small.
2	She hasn't got a	☐ sofa.	☐ bed.	☐ chair.
3	The elephant's name is	☐ Sammy.	☐ Andy.	☐ Piggy.
4	Ava's favourite place is	☐ her bed.	☐ her chair.	☐ her desk.
5	At her desk Ava	☐ listens to music.	☐ talks to Ollie.	☐ talks on the phone.
6	Ava has got lots of books	☐ about music.	☐ about dogs.	☐ about skateboarding.

2b wordbank: at home p. 158

Write about your room. You can use words from the boxes.

My room is ______________________ big, small, nice

There is ______________________ a chair, a bed, a lamp

There isn't ______________________ a sofa, a photo, a laptop

There are ______________________ clothes, comics, two posters

I have got ______________________ a football, a skateboard, a hamster

I haven't got ______________________ a dog, a desk, a lot of books

LANGUAGE HELP Personalpronomen

Anstatt ein Nomen mehrmals zu verwenden, kannst du es durch ein Personalpronomen ersetzen.
Singular: *I, you, he, she, it* Plural: *we, you, they*

Beispiele: *Megan is from Notting Hill. She is eleven.* *I've got a football. It is new.*
Leo and I are twins. We are twelve. *Apples and bananas are fruit. They are good for you.*

Ava and her family

3

Find the correct pronouns[1]. Underline the people and things in the right colour.

mum · Noah and Joshua · Ollie · dad · ball · blue house · Ava · three skateboards

he she it they

1 **pronoun** - Fürwort, Pronomen

Joshua

4 grammar: be p.166

Complete Joshua's sentences with words from the box.

is · are not · are · am · am not · am · is not

1 Hi! I ______ Joshua, Ava's little brother.

2 I ______ five years old, I ______ six.

3 I love Ollie, our dog, he ______ so nice.

4 Ava and my brother Noah ______ always nice.

5 Our house ______ big.

6 We ______ a happy family!

Ava and her brothers

5 grammar: have got p. 167

What have the children got? What have they not got? Complete the sentences with words from the box.

has not got · have got · have not got · has got

1 Ava *has got* a small room.

2 She ______ a sofa.

3 She ______ a dog.

4 She ______ a laptop.

5 She ______ a red bed.

6 She ______ books about music.

7 Noah and Joshua *have not got* a cat.

8 They ______ a blue house.

9 They ______ a big TV.

10 They ______ a small garden.

11 They ______ a sister.

12 They ______ books about cats.

Practise reading

Tipp 1
Bevor du einen Text liest, sieh dir die Überschrift an und überlege, worum es gehen könnte.

Harry and Lily

6a

The title of this text is "Harry and Lily". What could the text be about? Tick ✓ two things.

☐ things they have got ☐ things they like ☐ their teachers

6b audio 1/12

Now read the text. Can you find the information you expected[1]? Underline it.

Harry: Lily and I are new in Notting Hill. We live here with our two mums.

This is our room. Lily's got a big bed, it's her favourite place.

Lily's got a lot of things – a skateboard, books and a lot of funny socks. But she can never find them!

We love playing board games, so we've got a lot of them.

Lily: We've got two rabbits. Double is brown and Trouble is black and white. They are very sweet! They've got a blue cage.

Harry likes football. He's a big Chelsea fan and he's got a lot of posters. Harry also likes music. He's got a red guitar. He plays every evening. His favourite music is rock music and it's really loud.

1 **the information you expected** - die Informationen, die du erwartet hast

PRACTISE READING

Hat **Tipp 1** dir geholfen, den Text zu verstehen? ◯ ja ◯ teilweise ◯ nein

More about Harry and Lily

7

What do you know about Harry and Lily? Make notes.

Harry and Lily are: ______

They have got: ______

______

Tarek's room

8a CHOOSE YOUR LEVEL audio 1/13

I Listen to Tarek in TB7b again. Underline the correct words.

1 I live in Notting Hill with my *mum / dad*.
2 I *go skateboarding / play hockey* in the park.
3 I'm in a *hockey / football* team.
4 My uncle's got a *rabbit / cat*.

II Listen to Tarek again. Complete the sentences.

1 Tarek loves ______________ .
2 He goes skateboarding in the ______________ .
3 Tarek is a ______________ Arsenal fan.
4 Hip hop is his favourite ______________ .
5 There are ______________ posters in his room.

III Listen to Tarek again. What does he say about reading? ... sports? ... music? ... pets? Take notes.

____
____
____
____
____
____
____
____
____

8b skill: mediation p. 145

Look at Tarek's cat poster. What can you understand? Take notes in German.

There are 500 million cats in the world.
Some cats eat apples and bananas.
The oldest cat in the world was 38 years old.
How high can cats jump? More than two metres!
Cats can drink seawater.
In 1963 a cat went to space.
There are 2 million cat videos on the Internet.

____
____
____
____
____
____
____
____
____
____

The things I like and do not like

9

Rewrite the poem. You can use words with the same colour.

Football, burgers,
chocolate cake,
computers, puppies,
rap music, steak
loud and cool music,
riding my bike,
these are all
the things I like.
Homework, spinach,
stinky smells,
the way my sister
always yells,
shopping with my mum,
a ten-mile hike,
these are the things
I do not like.

swimming · tennis · …

pizza · ice cream · …

lemon · apple · …

Sundays · T-shirts · …

rabbits · tigers · …

pop · rock · …

carrots · broccoli · …

brother · cousin · …

cleaning my bike · singing with a mike[1] · …

1 **mike** – Mikro (Mikrofon)

All about Kai

10a video 2

Watch the video clip in TB11a again. What do you understand? Take notes.

How old is Kai?

Where is he from?

Family?

Room?

Hobbies?

Food?

Pets?

Best friend?

10b CHOOSE YOUR TASK

Look at your notes in 10a for help.

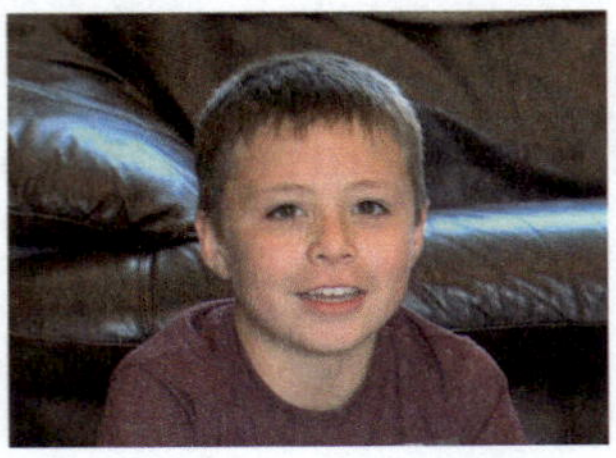

A **Make a word web about Kai.**
B **Talk about Kai. Record yourself.**
C **Make a quiz about Kai for a partner.**

Sound check

11a audio 1/15

Listen to the words and repeat them.

~~she~~ · like · about · all · back · we · look · great · too

black · ~~me~~ · gate · bike · ball · who · three · book · out

11b

Listen again. Match the rhyming words. Write them down.

she – me ____________________
like – ____________________

11c audio 1/16

Listen and check your rhyming pairs.

Cindy and her room

12 CHOOSE YOUR LEVEL

Look at the photo and make notes.
Talk about it and record yourself.
Edit your recording.

You can say:
I can see …
She's got …
The girl likes …
There is …
There are …

Say four or more sentences.
Say eight or more sentences.
Say ten or more sentences.

About me and my things TARGET TASK SUPPORT

13 wordbank: about me p. 151, family p. 160, skill: presentations p. 146

1 Make notes for your presentation.

my family: ______

my pet(s): ______

what I like: ______

my hobbies: ______

my favourite things: ______

______

2 Complete the sentences. Choose the sentences you want to use in your presentation.

Hello everybody, today I want to tell you about me and my things.

In my family there are ______

______.

My family: that's me and ______

______.

I live in ______.

I've got a pet. It's a ______.

Its name is ______.

Its colour is ______.

My pet and I like to ______

I haven't got a pet.

I really like ______.

And I like my ______.

I like ______ a lot.

My hobby is ______.

My hobbies are ______.

My favourite thing is ______.

I've got ______ favourite things.

This is my ______.

Here it is.

I haven't got a favourite thing.

Tipp: Eine Präsentation vorbereiten

1 Mache dir Notizen für deine Präsentation.
2 Formuliere deine Sätze und bitte einen Partner oder eine Partnerin um Feedback.
3 Übe deine Präsentation zuerst alleine.
4 Dann übe mit einem Partner oder einer Partnerin. Denke daran, langsam, laut und deutlich zu sprechen. Schaut einander beim Sprechen an.

In Notting Hill

1a audio 1/17

Listen to the names of the places. Repeat them.

Notting Hill Gate Station · Portobello Road Market · The Gate Picturehouse · Electric Cinema · Biscuiteers · Notting Hill Carnival

1b

Read the information in TB1b again. Tick ✓ true or false.

		true	false
1	You can't travel to Notting Hill on the underground.	☐	☐
2	The underground is fast and easy.	☐	☐
3	Portobello Road Market is a restaurant.	☐	☐
4	You can buy clothes and food there.	☐	☐
5	There are no cinemas in Notting Hill.	☐	☐
6	There is a Kids' Club at the Electric Cinema.	☐	☐
7	At Biscuiteers you can try something new.	☐	☐
8	You can't take your personal biscuit home.	☐	☐
9	Notting Hill Carnival is every year in February.	☐	☐
10	People watch the parade and listen to the music.	☐	☐

Challenge: **Correct the false sentences.**

LANGUAGE HELP — Nomen und Eigennamen

Im Deutschen schreibt man Nomen immer groß. Im Englischen schreibt man sie klein.
Beispiele: *Haus – house*

Im Englischen schreibt man nur Eigennamen groß, zum Beispiel von Tagen und Monaten, Orten und Straßen und Personen.
Beispiele: *Monday, April, Notting Hill, Portobello Road, Ava*

A trip to Notting Hill

2 skill: mediation p.145

Imagine your parents are planning a trip to Notting Hill. Answer their questions in German.

1 Ist die U-Bahn eine gute Möglichkeit, nach Notting Hill zu kommen? Warum?

2 Warum lohnt es sich, den Markt auf der Portobello Road zu besuchen?

3 Kinobesuche in London sollen sehr teuer sein. Können wir trotzdem gehen?

4 Ist Biscuiteers auch etwas für Erwachsene? Warum?

5 Warum soll sich ein Besuch im August besonders lohnen?

Let's text Ava

3a

Lily and Harry text Ava. Number the sentences in a good order.

A Please! ☺
B Can U take us on a tour?
C See you, bye.
D There is so much to do around Notting Hill.
E Hello Ava.
F We really want to see it all!
G How are U?

1	*E*
2	
3	
4	
5	
6	
7	

3b

Read the text message to a partner. Compare your texts.

3c CHOOSE YOUR TASK

A **Make a word snake about Notting Hill for a partner.**
B **Write Ava's answer to Harry and Lily.**
C **Write a text message about places you want to see in Notting Hill.**

Sound check

4a audio 1/18

Listen to the words and repeat them.

good · put · to · neighbourhood · book · football · would · look · foot · two

4b

Underline the different spellings for the sound /u/. Write them down.

oo, ______________________________

In the neighbourhood

5 CHOOSE YOUR LEVEL audio 1/19, skill: listening p. 141

Listen to Ameera.

I Tick ✓ the words you hear.

☐ park	→	☐ playground	→	☐ school	→	☐ garden
☐ shop	→	☐ restaurant	→	☐ cafés	→	☐ supermarket
☐ market	→	☐ skate park	→	☐ cinema	→	☐ swimming pool

II Listen to Ameera. Tick ✓ the correct sentence endings.

1 Ameera's favourite place is	☐ her street.	☐ her neighbourhood.	☐ the park.
2 At the park there is	☐ a playground.	☐ a small shop.	☐ a bus stop.
3 Next to her house there is	☐ a market.	☐ a small shop.	☐ a playground.
4 Ameera helps with the shopping	☐ on Tuesdays.	☐ on Fridays.	☐ on Saturdays.
5 At the cinema they watch	☐ new films.	☐ old films.	☐ lots of films.

III Listen to Ameera. Tick ✓ the correct sentences.

1 ☐ There is a playground in the park.
☐ There are a lot of dogs in the park.

2 ☐ Ameera goes to the small shop to buy sweets.
☐ Ameera goes to the market to buy sweets.

3 ☐ The cafés and the supermarket are next to the park.
☐ The cafés and the supermarket are in her street.

4 ☐ On Fridays Ameera and her dad go shopping.
☐ On Fridays Ameera and her dad go to the cinema.

5 ☐ The market is on Saturdays.
☐ The market is on Fridays.

6 ☐ They haven't got a supermarket in their neighbourhood.
☐ They haven't got a swimming pool in their neighbourhood.

Around here

6a

Look at the map. Match the questions and answers.

1 Is there a museum?	Yes, there is.
2 Is there a skatepark?	Yes, there is.
3 Are there schools?	No, there isn't.
4 Is there a fish and chip shop?	No, there aren't.
5 Are there markets?	Yes, there are.

6b grammar: be questions p. 168

Write down more questions about the map. Write down the answers, too.

+ On the map you can see:	**– On the map you can't see:**
a museum · a park · two schools · a café · two small shops · a fish and chip shop	a zoo · cinemas · swimming pools · playgrounds · a skatepark · markets

Is there a zoo? ______ ______

Are there ______ ______

Is there ______ ______

Is there ______ ______

Are there ______ ______

6c

Look at the map and make notes. Talk about it and record yourself. Edit the recording.

A tour of Notting Hill

7a grammar: be questions p. 168

Read TB6b again. Match the questions and the answers.

1 Are the friends on Portobello Road? — Yes, she is.
2 Is Lily ready for the tour? — No, it isn't.
3 Are Sarah and Olivia Ava's mums? — Yes, they are.
4 Is the market boring? — Yes, they are.
5 Are the T-shirts great? — No, there isn't.
6 Is there a flyer for the Kid's Club? — No, they aren't.

Challenge: Write more questions. Swap with a partner and answer your partner's questions.

____

____

____

7b grammar: be questions p. 168

Read TB6b again. Answer the questions.

1 Where are the friends? ______________________
2 What is special about the fish and chip shop? ______________________
3 Who has got two mums? ______________________
4 Where can you find lots of stalls? ______________________
5 What has Ava's favourite stall got? ______________________
6 Where is the flyer from? ______________________

A word snake

8

Find the words for places in the word snake.

schoolstallundergroundmarketparkstreetmuseumplaceshopcinema

Practise reading

Tipp 2

Es gibt viele Wörter, die im Englischen und im Deutschen ähnlich oder sogar gleich sind. Es kann helfen, nach solchen Wörtern zu schauen, wenn du einen Text liest.

A flyer

9a audio 1/21

Read the flyer from BaySixty6 again. Circle the words that are the same or similar in German[1] (or another language you know).

BaySixty6 – A skater's paradise

The only indoor skate park in London!

Are you an inline skater?

A skateboarder? A BMX biker?

BaySixty6 is fun for everyone!

- lessons for beginners
- special events for professionals

Where? 56–66 Acklam Road

When? Open daily from 12 to 9

How much? £6 per person per session

1 **the words that are the same or similar in German** – die Wörter, die auf Deutsch gleich oder ähnlich sind

9b

Write the words in the lists.

skater	*Skater*

9c skill: mediation p. 145

Use your list to say in German what the flyer is about.

PRACTISE READING

Hat **Tipp 2** dir geholfen, den Text zu verstehen? ◯ ja ◯ teilweise ◯ nein

Places in Notting Hill

10a CHOOSE YOUR LEVEL grammar: be questions p. 168

I Answer the questions.

~~Yes, they~~ are. · No, they aren't. · Yes, it is. · Yes, it is. · No, it isn't. · Yes, it is. · No, they aren't.

1 Are the friends in Holland Park? *Yes, they are.*
2 Is Holland Park a good place to relax? ______
3 Is the Japanese garden beautiful? ______
4 Are the friends in the museum? ______
5 Is Wonderlab boring? ______
6 Is the weather nice? ______

II Fill in the right question words.

1 *Where* are the children? In Holland Park.
2 ______ is in Holland Park? A beautiful Japanese garden.
3 ______ is Wonderlab? At the Science Museum.
4 ______ doesn't like bats? Harry.
5 ______ is the next live show? At four o'clock.
6 ______ is too nice to be indoors? The weather.

III Write questions for the answers.

1 *Where are the friends?* In Holland Park.
2 ______ A good place to relax.
3 ______ A Japanese garden and a cafeteria.
4 ______ A special lab at the Science Museum.
5 ______ At four o'clock.
6 ______ Getting some ice cream.

10b

Answer the questions. Write down the places.
Where can you …

watch a parade? *At the Notting Hill Carnival.* → eat the best fish and chips? ______
buy cool things? ______ → go on bat walks? ______
watch films? ______ → learn to skate? ______

Welcome

What's in the street? (Seite 4)

1a: Individuelle Lösung

1b: 1 yes **2** no **3** yes **4** no **5** yes

1c: Beispiellösung:

1 bus, cap, strawberry, cherry **2** car, cap, shopping bag, pair of jeans **3** taxi, jacket, bin, table **4** house, helmet, backpack, skirt

5 T-shirt, skateboard, handbag, tree **6** house, sweatshirt, hat, van

1d: food: apples, carrots **animals:** dog, cat **people:** girl, boy, child **other words:** house, bike, car, bus stop, park

1e: Beispiellösung:

food: ice cream, hamburger, chocolate, orange **animals:** parrot, bird, hamster, goldfish **people:** woman, father, baby, friend **other words:** motorbike, window, shop, street

Ice cream flavours (Seite 5-6)

2a: mango, orange, banana, lemon, strawberry, vanilla, cherry, chocolate

2b: 1 vanilla, strawberry **2** cherry **3** orange, lemon

2c: 3, 6, 5, 2, 4, 1 oder: **1** touch your nose **2** touch your toes **3** close one eye **4** jump up high **5** clap your hands **6** stamp your feet

At the ice cream van (Seite 6)

3a: 1 skateboard **2** places **3** welcome **4** please

3b: Ava: Sorry, just a minute. Welcome to Notting Hill then.

Harry: That's a nice skateboard. I'm new around here.

Harry meets Ava (Seite 7)

4a: 1 Harry **2** Ava **3** Joshua **4** Tarek **5** Noah oder: Noah and Tarek **6** Lily oder: Lily, Ava, and Harry

4b: 1 Do you skateboard? – Yes, I do. **2** Where do you go skateboarding? – In the park.

3 Where are you from? – I'm from Brighton.

4 What's your name? – I'm Harry. **5** How old are you? – I'm eleven. **6** Can I have your phone number? – Sure. It's 07984631205.

4c: 1 07694183256 **2** 07136459283 **3** 07840561192 **4** 07374106805

The next day (Seite 8)

5a: 1 Lily **2** Harry **3** Tarek **4** Ava **5** Noah

5b: 1 sister **2** brother **3** meet **4** Notting Hill **5** old **6** eleven **7** twelve **8** go

5c: 1 Lily and Ava **2** Tarek **3** Harry **4** Noah **5** Lily

Hi, what's your name? (Seite 9)

6a: 2 Hi, my name is Jake. **4** I'm from London. **6** I'm eleven. **8** I've got one sister. **10** Her name is Rosalie. **12** She's twelve.

6b: 1 name **2** two brothers **3** ten **4** six and eight **5** very good **6** name **7** black and white

Ava's little brother (Seite 9)

7: 1 My name is Joshua. **2** I'm from London. oder: I'm from Notting Hill. **3** I'm six. **4** I've got a sister and a brother. **5** Chocolate.

Welcome Check out (Seite 10-11)

1: You come and say: Hi. Nice to meet you. Hello. Good morning. **You go and say:** Bye. Goodbye. See you tomorrow.

2: 1 What's your name? **2** How old are you? **3** Where are you from? **4** What's the best ice cream flavour? **5** Can I have your phone number?

3: Individuelle Lösung

4: Beispiellösung:

Mia: This is my friend Bill and that is my sister Hanah. **Leo:** This is my friend Alice and that is my brother Frank.

5a: 1 Minnie: 07423896014

2 Jacob: 07219905765

5b: 1 oh-one-five-four-five-oh-eight-seven-nine-oh-eight **2** oh-one-six-five-eight-eight-oh-one-seven-nine-five **3** oh-one-nine-six-five-oh-three-two-eight-oh-four

Unit 1A

In Ava's room (Seite 12)

1a: Individuelle Lösung

1b: Beispiellösung:

There is a bed. There is a green chair. There is a laptop. There is an elephant. There is an apple. There is a glass. There is a ball. There are books. There are three skateboards. There are three cuddly toys. There are clothes. There are shoes. There are socks.

1c: her house: blue, small garden, Notting Hill **her hobbies:** playing computer games, skateboarding **her family:** mum, dad, two brothers **Ollie:** always hungry, four, carrots

1c Challenge: Beispiellösung:

her house: not big, I like it. **her hobbies:** three skateboards **her family:** no sister **Ollie:** lots of tricks, a red ball, spaghetti

Ava (Seite 13)

2a I: room, sofa, name, friends, laptop, skateboarding

2a II: 1 true **2** false **3** true **4** false **5** true

2a III: 1 small **2** sofa **3** Sammy **4** her desk **5** listens to music **6** about dogs

2b: Beispiellösung:

My room is small. There is a bed. There isn't a photo. There are clothes and a lot of books. I have got a football. I haven't got a computer.

Ava and her family (Seite 14)

3: he (orange)**:** Ollie, dad **she** (grün)**:** mum, Ava **it** (blau)**:** ball, blue house **they** (lila)**:** Noah and Joshua, three skateboards

Joshua (Seite 14)

4: 1 am **2** am not, am **3** is **4** are not **5** is not **6** are

Ava and her brothers (Seite 14)

5: 1 has got **2** has not got **3** has got **4** has got **5** has not got **6** has not got **7** have not got **8** have got **9** have not got **10** have got **11** have got **12** have not got

Practise reading: Harry and Lily (Seite 15)

6a: things they have got, things they like

6b: Beispiellösung:

Harry: Lily's got a big bed. Lily's got a lot of things – a skateboard, books and a lot of funny socks. We love playing board games, so we've got a lot of them.

Lily: We've got two rabbits. Harry likes football. He's got a lot of posters. Harry also likes music. He's got a red guitar.

More about Harry and Lily (Seite 15)

7: Beispiellösung:

Harry and Lily are: twins, brother and sister, eleven, from Brighton, new in Notting Hill

They have got: skateboards, two mums, one bedroom, two rabbits: Double and Trouble

Tarek's room (Seite 16)

8a I: 1 dad **2** go skateboarding **3** hockey **4** cat

8a II: 1 reading **2** park **3** big **4** music **5** animal

8a III: Beispiellösung: **reading:** loves reading, has got a lot of books, fantasy stories are the best **sports:** likes hockey, football, skateboarding, goes skateboarding in the park, is a big Arsenal fan, is in a hockey team **music:** doesn't like pop music, likes hip hop **pets:** hasn't got a pet, likes cats a lot, his uncle has got a cat, has got animal posters in his room

8b: Beispiellösung: Auf dem Poster stehen 7 lustige Tatsachen über Katzen. Es gibt 500 Millionen Katzen auf der Welt. Manche Katzen fressen Obst. Die älteste Katze wurde 38 Jahre alt. Katzen können mehr als zwei Meter hoch springen und sie können Salzwasser trinken. 1963 ist eine Katze in den Weltraum gereist. Im Internet gibt es über 2 Millionen Katzenvideos.

The things I like and do not like (Seite 17)

9: Beispiellösung:

Swimming, pizza, apple cake, Sundays, rabbits, pop music, steak, loud and cool music, riding my bike, these are all the things I like. Homework, carrots, stinky smells, the way my brother always yells, shopping with my mum, singing with a mike, these are the things I do not like.

All about Kai (Seite 17-18)
10a: How old is Kai? eleven **Where is he from?** Portsmouth **Family?** mum, dad, sister (Oakley) **Room?** books, DVDs, computer games, toy cars, posters **Hobbies?** football, basketball, swimming **Food?** loves crips, hates bananas **Pets?** fish (Shakeel, Jaws, Psy), would love a dog **Best friend?** Louis
10bA: Individuelle Lösung
10bB: Beispiellösung:
Kai is a boy from Portsmouth. He is eleven years old. He lives with his family, that's his mum and dad and his sister. In his room there are books, DVDs, computer games, toy cars and posters. His favourite hobby is swimming. He loves crisps and hates bananas. He has got three fish with funny names. He would love a dog. His best friend is Louis. Kai and Louis like riding their bikes.
10bC: Individuelle Lösung

Sound check (Seite 18)
11a: Individuelle Lösung
11b: she – me, like – bike, about – out, all – ball, back – black, we – three, look – book, great – gate, too – who
11c: Individuelle Lösung

Cindy and her room (Seite 18)
12: Beispiellösung:
I can see a girl. She sits on a sofa in her room. The sofa is red. The girl has got a red T-shirt and jeans. She likes red things. The room is nice. She's got a guitar. There is a picture of an elephant. She likes cuddly toys. There are many posters. I can also see a table. There is a cup on the table. I can see an exercise book on the sofa.

About me and my things (Seite 19)
13: Individuelle Lösungen

Unit 1B
In Notting Hill (Seite 20)
1a: Individuelle Lösung
1b: 1 false **2** true **3** false **4** true **5** false **6** true **7** true **8** false **9** false **10** true
Challenge: 1 You can travel to Notting Hill on the underground. **3** Portobello Road Market is a market. **5** There are many cinemas in Notting Hill. **8** You can take your personal biscuit home. **9** Notting Hill Carnival is every year in August.

A trip to Notting Hill (Seite 21)
2: Beispiellösung:
1 Ja, weil es schnell und einfach ist. **2** Es ist einer der besten Märkte in London. **3** Ja, im Gate Picturehouse gibt es spezielle Karten für Kinder. **4** Ja, es ist etwas für alle, die kreativ sind. **5** Weil im August der Notting Hill Carnival stattfindet.

Let's text Ava (Seite 21)
3a: Beispiellösung:
1E, 2G, 3D, 4F, 5B, 6A, 7C
3b+c: Individuelle Lösungen

Sound check (Seite 22)
4a: Individuelle Lösung
4b: good, put, to, neighbourhood, book, football, would, look, foot, two; oo, u, o, ou, wo

In the neighbourhood (Seite 22)
5 I: park, playground, shop, cafés, supermarket, market, cinema, swimming pool
5 II: 1 the park **2** a playground **3** a small

shop **4** on Fridays **5** old films
5 III: 1 There is a playground in the park. **2** Ameera goes to the small shop to buy sweets. **3** The cafés and the supermarket are in her street. **4** On Fridays, Ameera and her dad go shopping. **5** The market is on Saturdays. **6** They haven't got a swimming pool in their neighbourhood.

Around here (Seite 23)
6a: 1 Yes, there is. **2** No, there isn't. **3** Yes, there are. **4** Yes, there is. **5** No, there aren't.
6b: Beispiellösung:
Is there a zoo? – No, there isn't. Are there two small shops? – Yes, there are. Is there a skatepark? – No, there isn't. Is there a café? – Yes, there is. Are there cinemas? – No, there aren't.
6c: Individuelle Lösung

A tour of Notting Hill (Seite 24)
7a: 1 Yes, they are. **2** Yes, she is. **3** No, they aren't. **4** No, it isn't. **5** Yes, they are. **6** No, there isn't.
Challenge: Beispiellösung:
Is Milligan's Fish&Chips the best in Notting Hill? – Yes, it is. Are there many stalls on Portobello Road? – Yes, there are. Is the T-shirt five pounds? – No, it isn't.
7b: Beispiellösung:
1 in Notting Hill **2** It's their favourite. oder: It's the best. **3** Lily and Harry **4** at Portobello Road Market **5** great second-hand T-shirts **6** the skate park oder: BaySixty6

A word snake (Seite 24)
8: school / stall / underground / market / park / street / museum / place / shop / cinema

Practise reading: A flyer (Seite 25)
9a: skater, paradise, skate park, in, inline skater, skateboarder, biker, beginner, special, event, professional, person, session
9b: skater – Skater, paradise – Paradies, skate park – Skatepark, in – in, inline skater – Inlineskater, skateboarder – Skateboarder, biker – Biker, beginner – Beginner/in, special – speziell, event – Event, professional – Profi, person – Person, session – Session
9c: Individuelle Lösung

Places in Notting Hill (Seite 26)
10a I: 1 Yes, they are. **2** Yes, it is. **3** Yes, it is. **4** No, they aren't. **5** No, it isn't. **6** Yes, it is.
10a II: 1 Where **2** What **3** Where **4** Who **5** When **6** What
10a III: 1 Where are the friends? **2** What is Holland Park? **3** What is there at Holland Park? **4** What is Wonderlab? **5** When is the live show? **6** What is a brilliant idea?
10b: Beispiellösung:
at the Notting Hill Carnival, at Milligan's, at Portobello Road Market, at the Ecology Centre, at the Gate Picturehouse, at BaySixty6

Great places in your area (Seite 27)
11.1: what – was, where – wo, when – wann, how – wie, how much – wie viel
11.2-4: Individuelle Lösung

Unit 1 Check out (Seite 28-29)
1: 1 Alisha has got an Arsenal poster. **2** She hasn't got a sister. **3** She has got a cat. **4** Roy and Arlo haven't got an Arsenal poster. **5** They have got a sister. **6** They haven't got a cat.
2: name: Lewis **lives in:** London **family:** dad, sister **pet:** a cat **likes:** his room, skateboarding, pizza, apples **hates:** carrots, strawberry ice cream **hobbies:** playing computer games, reading comics **favourite things:** skateboard, computer
3: Beispiellösung:
Hi, I'm Ella / Paul. I'm from Oxford in England. I live with my parents and my brother. I've got two hamsters and three cats. I like films about

animals and vanilla pudding. My hobbies are singing and reading. My favourite things are my fantasy books and my tablet.
4: 1 false **2** false **3** true **4** true **5** false
5: Is there a cinema? – Yes, there is. Are there museums? – No, there aren't. Is there a market? – No, there isn't. Are there cafés? – Yes, there are.
6: Beispiellösung:
There is a big playground in my neighbourhood. It is in a park. It is open daily. I go skateboarding there with my friends. It is my favourite place. It is cool.

Unit 2A
Pack your schoolbag (Seite 30)
1a: pencil case, scissors, pencil sharpener, folders, notepad, ruler, exercise books, calculator, glue
1b: Individuelle Lösung

School things in Tarek's room (Seite 30-31)
2a: 1 folders **2** exercise books **3** schoolbag **4** pencil case **5** pens **6** pencils **7** eraser **8** pencil sharpener **9** ruler **10** calculator
2b I: folders, exercise books
2b II: pens, pencils, eraser, pencil sharpener
2b III: folders, exercise books, pens, pencils, eraser, pencil sharpener, ruler, calculator

Check the teacher's bag (Seite 31)
3: a folder, an English book, a pencil case, a pen, a calculator, pencils, exercise books
3 Challenge: Beispiellösung:
two apples, chocolate, a photo of a dog, a phone, a water bottle, a lunchbox, sunglasses

Practise reading: Assembly (Seite 32)
4a: Beispiellösung:
Ich sehe einen großen Raum mit einer Bühne. Es sieht aus wie eine Aula bei einer Schülerversammlung. Vorne steht ein Lehrer und redet. Es ist neun Uhr. Es gibt einen Beamer und eine Leinwand. Darauf steht "Willkommen an der Holland Park Schule". Viele Jungen und Mädchen sitzen auf den Stühlen. Sie tragen Schuluniformen.
4b: Beispiellösung:
boys and girls, Welcome to Holland Park School, headteacher, assembly, nine o'clock
4c: 1 the new school **2** at the notice board

Eat your spaghetti! (Seite 33)
5: Beispiellösungen:
Bild 1: 1 Don't talk. **2** Open your pencil cases. **3** Take out your pens. **Bild 2: 1** Listen to the song. **2** Look at my new shoes. **3** Don't shout at me. **Bild 3: 1** Don't eat here. **2** Open the door, please. **3** Don't run here. **Bild 4: 1** Eat your spaghetti. **2** Don't play with the ball here. **3** Look at my homework.

Sound check (Seite 33)
6: mum, bus, much, funny, number, but, club

What's the time? (Seite 34)
7a+b: Individuelle Lösungen
7c: 1 It's quarter past nine. oder: It's nine fifteen. **2** It's half past four. oder: It's four thirty. **3** It's six forty (pm). oder: It's twenty to seven (pm). **4** It's ten past three.
7d: Individuelle Lösung
7e: Beispiellösung:
Zu 9:45h sagt man auf Deutsch meist "viertel vor zehn". In manchen Regionen sagt man aber auch "dreiviertel zehn". Im Englischen gibt es dafür keine Entsprechung. Man sagt meist "quarter to ten".
Zu 11:30 sagt man auf Deutsch "elf Uhr dreißig" oder "halb zwölf". Im Englischen gibt es für halb zwölf keine direkte Entsprechung. Man sagt "eleven thirty" oder "half past eleven".

School subjects (Seite 35)
8a: French / maths / art/ English / science /

geography / PE / history / ICT / music / RE
8b: Individuelle Lösung
8c: Beispiellösung:
My favourite subject is PE because I like sports. I like maths because I'm really good at it. I also like RE because our teacher, Mrs Jakobi, is really nice. I don't like music because I don't like to sing in class. And I don't like history because it's boring.

Spelling fun (Seite 35)
9: Individuelle Lösungen

***A* or *an*?** (Seite 36)
10a: a computer, an eraser, a ruler, an orange ball, an activity, a pencil, an open book, a folder, an English teacher, an office
10b: Individuelle Lösung

Classroom questions (Seite 36)
11: 1 What page please? **2** Where is your pencil sharpener? **3** Can you spell calculator please? **4** What is homework in German? **5** Can I borrow a ruler please?

More spelling (Seite 36)
12a: 1 box **2** child **3** city **4** class **5** foot **6** life **7** man
12b: 1 boxes **2** children **3** cities **4** classes **5** feet **6** lives **7** men

A classroom board game (Seite 37)
13.1+2: Individuelle Lösungen
13.3: 1 Nimm eine Karte. **2** Lies die Karte vor. **3** Du bist dran. **4** Würfle. **5** Würfle noch einmal. **6** Du musst aussetzen. **7** Gehe drei Felder zurück. **8** Gehe zwei Felder vor. **9** Fang von vorne an.

Unit 2B
Practise reading: What's on at Holland Park School? (Seite 38)
1a: Individuelle Lösung
1b: Poster 1: What? – Cooking club When? – Tuesdays, 4:15pm-5:45pm Where? – school kitchen Who? – all students
Poster 2: What? – Football team When? – Wednesdays, 4:00pm-5:30pm Where? – at the gym Who? – you

A club for Nina and Freddie (Seite 38)
2: drama club
2 Challenge: Individuelle Lösung

Clubs at Holland Park School (Seite 39)
3a I-III: 1 read one new book every month **2** in the school kitchen **3** on Saturdays **4** everybody **5** at the science lab **6** your instrument **7** Mrs Baker **8** every Friday from 4pm to 6pm
3b: 1 The book club reads one new book every month. **2** The football team practises every Wednesday. **3** The school band meets with instruments every Friday. **4** The science club does exciting experiments on Thursdays. **5** The football team plays matches on Saturdays.

The day of the week (Seite 39)
4: 1 Sunday **2** Wednesday **3** Thursday, Saturday **4** Monday **5** Friday **6** Tuesday, Thursday
4 Challenge: Individuelle Lösung

That doesn't sound bad (Seite 40)
5a I: 1 says **2** says **3** sounds **4** goes
5a II: 1 says **2** says **3** likes **4** meet **5** goes **6** try
5a III: 1 doesn‘t play **2** doesn't like **3** says **4** doesn't sound **5** likes **6** meet **7** goes **8** try
5b: Beispiellösung:
1 I like the school band. **2** I don't like the drama club. **3** I think the science club is great. **4** The cooking club sounds great.
5 I don't want to try the football team.
6 The book club doesn't sound bad.

More school clubs (Seite 41)
6/A: What? Computer club **Who can come?**

boys and girls **When?** Tuesdays from 4pm to 5pm **Where?** in the computer room **Who is the teacher?** Ms Jameson
6/B+C: Individuelle Lösungen

Ava and Lily at school (Seite 41)
7: 1 Lily doesn't like team sports. **2** Noah says the science club is great. **3** At the science club they do experiments. **4** The science club doesn't sound bad. **5** Lunch before the book club isn't a problem. **6** Ava doesn't go to the science club. **7** Lily likes apple pie a lot. **8** The girls want to try the book club.

Sound check (Seite 41)
8a+b: Individuelle Lösungen

Tarek and his uncle (Seite 42)
9: 1 does **2** goes **3** teaches **4** plays **5** practises

All about school (Seite 42-43)
10a: 1 registration **2** school club **3** assembly **4** break **5** house **6** school uniform
10b I-III: 1 Die Lehrkraft ruft die Namen der Kinder auf. **2** Am Nachmittag kann man besondere Kurse besuchen. **3** Alle treffen sich morgens in der Aula. **4** die Zeit zum Essen und Trinken **5** Gruppen innerhalb der Schule mit eigenen Farben und Namen **6** die Schulkleidung mit dem Schulabzeichen darauf
10c: 1 grey pullover **2** black blazer **3** black trousers **4** black skirt **5** blue shirt **6** blue and grey tie **7** black shoes **8** black socks

A video chat with friends (Seite 43)
11 I: 1 she **2** they **3** he **4** they **5** they
11 II: 1 Yes, she does. **2** No, she doesn't. **3** Yes, he does. **4** Yes, they do. **5** No, they don't.
11 III: 1 No, she doesn't. **2** No, she doesn't. **3** Yes, they do. **4** Yes, she does. **5** No, they don't.

The rooms at school (Seite 44)
12a: 1 gym – do sports **2** assembly hall – meet for assembly **3** school kitchen – learn to cook **4** music room – play instruments **5** classroom – learn together **6** science lab – do experiments **7** library – read books **8** cafeteria – have lunch
12b: Beispiellösung:
1 Tarek learns to cook in the school kitchen. **2** Ava reads books in the library. **3** Noah and Lily do experiments in the science lab. **4** The students meet for assembly in the assembly hall. **5** The class meets in the classroom. **6** The students do sports in the gym.

Welcome to our school (Seite 44)
13: 1 before school **2** lunch **3** a T-shirt

Our school (Seite 45)
14: Individuelle Lösung

Unit 2 Check out (Seite 46-47)
1: + Read a lot of books. Do your homework. Have fun at school.
– Don't use your phone in class. Don't be late for the lesson. Don't forget your books.
2: 1 pencil case **2** exercise book **3** board **4** bookshelves **5** desk **6** schoolbag
3: 1 It's eight o'clock. **2** It's quarter past ten. **3** It's half past three. **4** It's quarter to ten. **5** It's twenty past six.
4: Tarek's uncle Sami goes to fitness class on Wednesdays. He meets his friends at the weekend. Jonah and Ellen practise with the school band on Tuesdays. They go to the library on Thusday afternoons.
5: 1 half past seven **2** registration **3** four lessons **4** twelve o'clock to twelve forty-five **5** two lessons **6** drama club
6: 1 Do you wear a school uniform? **2** Do you like your teachers? **3** When do you start school in the morning? **4** What is your favourite subject? **5** Do you go to a school club?

Unit 3A

Breakfast with Ava's family (Seite 48)

1a: cold food: tomatoes, butter, cereal, jam, chocolate spread, fruit **hot food:** bacon, eggs, (vegetarian) sausages, baked beans, (tomatoes), toast **drinks:** orange juice, coffee, tea, milk **things to set the table:** plates, cups, knives, forks, spoons

1a Challenge: Individuelle Lösung

1b: 1 true **2** false **3** false **4** false **5** true **6** false

1b Challenge: 2 Noah likes vegetarian sausages. <u>oder:</u> Mum likes tomatoes with her breakfast. **3** They need some cereal. **4** The children set the table. <u>oder:</u> Ava and Joshua set the table. **6** Noah never helps.

1c: 1 Yes, it is. **2** No, she doesn't. **3** No, they don't. **4** Yes, they do. **5** No, they aren't. **6** Yes, he is.

Different breakfasts (Seite 49)

2 I-III: Individuelle Lösungen

What time is it? (Seite 49)

3: 3, 5, 4, 1, 7, 8, 2, 6

Spot the difference (Seite 50)

4a: Individuelle Lösung

4b: one cup, one knife, one sausage, one toast, the butter, the orange juice, one banana

4c I-III: Beispiellösung:

On the table there is breakfast for two people. There are two large blue plates. On each plate there is an egg and baked beans, two sausages and (a piece of) toast. Each person has a knife and a fork, a blue cup and a glass. There is orange juice and tea to drink. There is also some milk for the tea. There is butter for the toast and jam. There are also two bananas. The breakfast looks yummy.

Full English breakfast (Seite 50-51)

5: Beispiellösung:

1 Beide Cafés bieten ein traditionelles englisches Frühstück an. **2** Diana's Café ist in der Stadtmitte, nicht weit entfernt von einem U-Bahnhof. Lucky Lunch ist in der Nähe von Holland Park. **3** Diana's Café hat Speck, Würstchen, Eier, gebackene Bohnen und gegrillte Tomaten. Bei Lucky Lunch wird nichts darüber gesagt. **4** Bei Lucky Lunch gibt es ein vegetarisches englisches Frühstück sowie Pfannkuchen mit Früchten. Bei Diana's Café steht dazu nichts. **5** Diana's Café ist wohl recht teuer, aber soll es wert sein. Bei Lucky Lunch steht, dass sie gutes Essen zu einem guten Preis anbieten. **6** Diana's Café hat viele Kaffeespezialitäten. Bei Lucky Lunch gibt es die Pfannkuchen mit Früchten als Spezialität zum Frühstück. **7** Manche Leute sagen, es sei der beste frische Orangensaft in London. **8** Diana's Café ist jeden Tag von 6 bis 13 Uhr geöffnet. Das würde also gehen. Lucky Lunch ist montags leider geschlossen.

Sound check (Seite 51)

6: The 's' sounds like the snake /s/.

A breakfast survey (Seite 51)

7 I: Mathilda: parents', avocado, sweet **Nick:** an egg, mum, like **Kerim:** grandma, orange juice, week

7 II: Beispiellösung:

1 Mathilda and her brother eat breakfast at their parents' café. **2** They don't eat the same things for breakfast. <u>oder:</u> They eat different things for breakfast. **3** Nick eats breakfast at home (before he does sports). **4** He only eats an egg and some toast. **5** Kerim's grandma makes the breakfast. **6** Kerim and his family have a full English breakfast.

7 III: Beispiellösung:

1 Mathilda has a favourite breakfast. She likes an egg and avocado sandwich. **2** Nick is not hungry in the morning. **3** Mathilda's brother, Nick, and Kerim and his family eat toast. **4** She thinks that an egg and some toast is not enough. **5** Kerim, his parents, his grandparents

and his sisters. **6** They talk about the last week and their plans for the next week.
7 Challenge: Individuelle Lösung

Bathroom words (Seite 52)
8: shower / clean / style / teeth / wash / brush / ears / bathroom / comb / hair / smelly

Noah in the bathroom (Seite 52)
9a: 1 Noah takes a shower. **2** He brushes his teeth. **3** Noah cleans his ears. **4** He combs his hair. **5** Perfection takes time.
9b: 1 Noah takes a shower after breakfast. **2** He washes his feet every day. **3** He styles his hair after the shower. **4** The family takes Ollie to the park. **5** Noah packs his schoolbag in the evening.
9 Challenge: Subjekt: Noah, He, He, The family, Noah **Verb:** takes, washes, styles, takes, packs **Objekt:** a shower, his feet, his hair, Ollie, his schoolbag **Ergänzung:** after breakfast. every day. after the shower. to the park. in the evening

They take him to the park (Seite 53)
10: 1 Noah takes it after breakfast. **2** He washes them every day. **3** He styles it after the shower. **4** The family takes him to the park. **5** Noah packs it in the evening.

Weekend activities (Seite 53)
11: Individuelle Lösung

More weekend activities (Seite 53)
12A/B: Individuelle Lösungen
12/C: Beispiellösung: Der Mann erzählt von der Zeit, als er noch ein Junge war. Im Winter haben er und sein Bruder im Wohnzimmer vor dem Kamin gespielt. Die besonderen Aktivitäten vor Weihnachten: Aus alten Weihnachtskarten Dekorationen für den Weihnachtsbaum zu basteln und Brot am Kaminfeuer zu rösten.

Practise reading: What a perfect day (Seite 54)
13a: Ava, Harry, Tarek, Lily, Noah
13b: a perfect day
13c: Beispiellösung:
Ava: sunshine, friends and watermelon
Harry: ice cream, I do what I want **Tarek:** I make lunch for my dad and my uncle, I play hockey with my friends, in the evening I stay up late **Lily:** I stay in bed all morning and read, I play with my rabbits, I go to a flea market, for dinner we go to the fish and chip shop, then we play board games **Noah:** pancakes for breakfast, I meet my friends in the park, we play football, eat pizza, in the afternoon we watch a film

My perfect day at the weekend (Seite 55)
14: Individuelle Lösungen

Unit 3B
Free time activities (Seite 56)
1: Individuelle Lösung

Favourite hobbies (Seite 56)
2a: cooking, skateboarding, music, playing the guitar, singing, playing an instrument, dancing, team sports
2b I-III: Ava: Ava can't cook. She likes skateboarding. She can do some tricks. Her best trick is the kickflip. **Tarek:** Tarek's favourite hobby is cooking. He goes to cooking club. He can cook lots of different things. His favourite is lasagna. **Harry:** Harry's hobby is music. He can play the guitar. He can't sing. His favourite music is rock music. He listens to music a lot. **Lily:** Lily likes music, too. She can't play an instrument. She can dance. Her favourite style is streetdance. She doesn't like teamsports.

A hobby survey (Seite 57)
3a+b: Individuelle Lösungen

Sound check (Seite 57)
4a: Individuelle Lösung
4b: Words with the long /i:/ sound are: team, meal, please, leave, read, speak, ice cream
4c: Individuelle Lösung

More fun activities (Seite 58)
5 I: 1 I can / can't swim. **2** I can / can't play basketball. **3** I can / can't play football.
4 I can / can't play hockey. **5** I can / can't do karate. **6** I can / can't ride a horse.
5 II: 1 can't **2** can **3** can't **4** can't **5** can **6** can't
5 III: 1 Bob can dance, but he can't play tennis.
2 Leila can ride a bike, but she can't play the guitar.
3 Eva can't climb a tree, but she can play football.
4 Fred can't play handball, but he can run fast.
5 Judy can draw pictures, but she can't sing.
6 Paul can't ice-skate, but he can jump very high.
5 Challenge: Individuelle Lösung

My favourite sport (Seite 58)
6 I-III: 1 Gracie: eleven **Amy:** fourteen **Sophia:** thirteen **2 Gracie:** dance **Amy:** football **Sophia:** hockey **3 Gracie:** every day **Amy:** twice a week **Sophia:** four times a week in winter **4 Gracie:** All you need is music. **Amy:** a football, uniform, special shoes **Sophia:** a hockey stick, a ball, protection for your teeth, hockey shoes, protection for your legs **5 Gracie:** likes to move to the music **Amy:** playing in a team is cool **Sophia:** it's a fast sport, it's good to play in a team with friends

Team table tennis (Seite 59)
7: 1 drei oder mehr **2** an einer Tischtennis-platte **3** man muss ausscheiden **4** Wer am Schluss übrig bleibt, gewinnt.

Anton's hobby (Seite 59)
8 I-III: Beispiellösung: I can see many different things like computer games, leaves and mugs. There are five different mugs. They are really nice, I like them. Anton's got a lot of cuddly toys. I can see a rabbit, a pig, a teddy bear, a duck, an elephant and something funny that is red and white. There are many books about horses. I think he likes horses. He collects postcards. There is a postcard of Paris. He has got stones and feathers. I have got stones and feathers, too. He also collects stickers. And there are some DVDs. I think he really likes comics. I like comics, too. Anton collects sea shells. I (also) collect sea shells. I don't collect posters.

Practise reading: Getting into the game (Seite 60-61)
9a-d: Individuelle Lösungen

Playing rugby (Seite 61)
10a: Individuelle Lösung
10b: 1 Rugby is a team sport. **2** In standard rugby, there are two teams of 15 players. **3** You play rugby on a rugby field. **4** You need a rugby ball. **5** The players can kick, throw and catch the ball. They can tackle other players to take the ball from them. **6** When a player puts the ball on or behind the other team's goal line, or kicks the ball over the field goal.

Another hobby (Seite 61)
11a: 60, 57, 18, 92, 12, 24, 30, 82, 17, 63
11b: 49 forty-nine, 68 sixty-eight, 86 eighty-six, 13 thirteen, 71 seventy-one, 33 thirty-three

Who can play? (Seite 62)
12: 1 Who can play hockey? **2** What can Ava do? **3** Where can't you swim? **4** When can we go home? **5** What can't Lars play?

Sound check (Seite 62)
13: There are different ways to say the letter "i".

Your favourite activity (Seite 62)
14 I-III: Individuelle Lösungen

Present a sport or hobby (Seite 63)
15: Individuelle Lösungen

Unit 3 Check out (Seite 64-65)
1: Individuelle Lösungen
2: Beispiellösung:
On Saturday at 9:30am Harry has breakfast with Tarek and his dad. At 5pm he watches a film at the Electric Cinema with Lily.
On Sunday at 1pm Harry has dinner at an Indian restaurant with his family. In the afternoon he plays board games with Ava and Lily.
3: 1 at her place **2** listen to music and play with the rabbits **3** at 2pm
4: Alfie can swim fast. He can climb high walls. He can draw pictures. Alfie can't make lunch. He can't ride a horse. He can't play rugby.
5: 1 gym **2** goal **3** ice rink **4** racket **5** athletics **6** swimming pool
6: 1 false **2** false **3** true **4** false **5** false **6** true

Unit 4A
Saturday afternoon (Seite 66)
1: 1 Tarek, Lily, Harry and Ava
2: Beispiellösung: It's raining.
3+4: Individuelle Lösungen

At Uncle Sami's house (Seite 66)
2 I-III: Beispiellösung:
1B, 2G, 3A, 4F, 5E, 6C, 7D, 8H

Getting ready for the game (Seite 67)
3: 1 She wants to ask her about buying snacks. **2** in the kitchen **3** at the corner shop **4** 20 pounds **5** at 7 o'clock **6** escape
3 Challenge: Beispiellösung:
Lily wants to find her mum. She wants to ask her about buying some snacks. Lily's mum is in the kitchen. Lily wants to buy snacks at the corner shop. Lily's mum gives her 20 pounds. Dinner is at 7 o'clock. Before dinner Lily and her friends have to escape.

The weather (Seite 67)
4a: Beispiellösung:
sun, sunny, nice, warm, hot, summer
rainy, cloud, wet weather, rain
wind, windy, cool, autumn
cold, ice cold, snow, frozen
4b: Individuelle Lösung

Questions (Seite 68)
5 I: 1 How **2** What **3** Who **4** Where **5** When
5 II: 1 How – Harry is eleven. **2** What – They have got rabbits. **3** Who – Tarek can cook.
4 Where – They go to Holland Park School.
5 When – School starts at twenty to nine.
5 III: Individuelle Lösung

Practise reading: In the corner shop (Seite 68-69)
6a: Beispiellösung: milk, pay, biscuits, please, ice cream, crisps, bottles, apples
6b: Individuelle Lösung
6c: Beispiellösung:
milk, pay, biscuits, please, ice cream, crisps, bottles, apples

Is that everything? (Seite 69-70)
7a: Is that everything? **S** How much are the crisps? **C** Hello! **B** They are over there, next to the apples. **S** The crisps are one pound forty. **S** How much is it? **C** Can I help you? **S** That's 7 pounds 80 pence, please. **S** Here you are. **B** Could I have a bottle of apple juice, please? **C** Thank you very much for your help. **C** You're welcome! **B** Have a nice evening. **B** Thanks a lot! **B** Excuse me. Where are the oranges, please? **C** Thank you. Bye, children! **S**
7b: Individuelle Lösung

At night at the corner shop (Seite 70)
8a+b: 1 The mice are between the carrots and the apples. **2** The mice are sitting on the

strawberries. **3** The mice are standing behind the water bottles. **4** The mice are in front of the fridge. **5** The mice are playing under the shelves. **6** The mice are sitting next to the cat.

Shopping for food (Seite 71)
9/A: Individuelle Lösung
9/B: milk, yoghurt, cheese, three red apples, bread
9/C: drei Äpfel, braunen Zucker, Mehl, Butter, Salz, Vanilleeis

A tidy bedroom (Seite 71)
10a: Individuelle Lösung
10b: 1 Harry's **2** Lily's **3** Lily and Harry's **4** Harry's **5** Lily and Harry's **6** Lily's

Your room (Seite 72)
11a: Individuelle Lösung
11b: 1 This is my bedroom. **2** I like my bedroom because ... **3** This is my bookcase where I keep ... **4** And this is where I do my homework. **5** This is my wardrobe. **6** And this is my bed. **7** Behind me is my favourite ... **8** Next to my ... is my schoolbag. **9** That was my room. I hope you liked it.
11c: Individuelle Lösung

Next to the door (Seite 72)
12 I-III: Individuelle Lösungen

Sound check (Seite 72)
13: Individuelle Lösung

Fun activities at home (Seite 73)
14: Individuelle Lösungen

Unit 4B
Jobs at home (Seite 74)
1: Beispiellösung:
bake a cake, clean the bathroom, do the cooking, do the shopping, tidy the living room, cook dinner, wash the plates, make the bed

Who says what? (Seite 74)
2: 1A, 2D, 3D, 4A, 5D, 6D, 7A, 8D

Mum's message (Seite 74)
3: buy some tomatoes, does the shopping, do the cooking, do the shopping for Granny, empty the dishwasher, go to the supermarket, empty the dishwasher
3 Challenge: Individuelle Lösung

A chores survey (Seite 75)
4a I-III: Individuelle Lösungen
4b: Rita's family: vacuum: dad / always, clean kitchen: dad / usually, tidy: sister / often
Ben's family: vacuum: mum / always, clean kitchen: mum / always, tidy: Ben / sometimes
Lotta's family: vacuum: mum / often, clean kitchen: grandpa / always, tidy: Lotta / always

Sound check (Seite 76)
5: do – does, go – goes, try – tries, empty – empties, guess – guesses, finish – finishes

Chores for the ghost family (Seite 76)
6a: 1 Billy sometimes cleans the cage in his bedroom. **2** Milly always vacuums the living room. **3** Vanilly usually sets the table in the kitchen. **4** Zilly often tidies the living room. **5** Pilly never cleans the bathroom.
6b: Individuelle Lösung

Where is Ollie? (Seite 77)
7: 1 Ollie is behind the laptop. **2** He is in the box. **3** He is on the skateboard. **4** He is in front of the shelves. **5** He is under the bed. **6** He is next to the schoolbag.

Don McClean in action (Seite 77)
8a: living room, bathroom, kitchen, bedroom
8b I-III: Beispiellösung:

Mr Dull has got a new robot. Its name is Don McClean. It can do all your chores for you. It is Mr Dull's birthday present. He is very happy with it! But today the robot starts moving around the living room and collecting the books from the shelves. It's throwing them on the floor! Then it is leaving the living room and going into the bathroom! Something is falling over. But the robot is not in the bathroom. It's in the kitchen. The cat is screaming. But Don McClean is already in the bedroom! A pillow comes flying into the kitchen! This robot is crazy.

Ollie's week (Seite 78-79)
9a: Beispiellösung:
Bild 1: skateboard, park **Bild 2:** dog school, friends, dogs **Bild 3:** kitchen, homework, garden **Bild 4:** kitchen, cooking, brother
Bild 5: kitchen, mum, living room, dad, sofa
9b+c: Individuelle Lösungen

The days of Ollie's week (Seite 79)
10a/A-C: Individuelle Lösungen
10b: Individuelle Lösung

What a day (Seite 80)
11 I: 1 Wednesday **2** spaghetti **3** garden
4 run **5** play **6** homework **7** eat **8** terrible
11 II: 1 Ollie loves Wednesdays. **2** Ollie wants to eat spaghetti with Ava. **3** Ava doesn't look happy when she comes home. **4** Ava has a lot of homework. **5** Ava shouts at Ollie.
11 III: Individuelle Lösung

More sorting (Seite 80)
12: rooms in the house: kitchen, bedroom **chores:** take out the rubbish, clean the bathroom **activities:** walk in the park, play a board game **days of the week:** Saturday, Wednesday
12 Challenge: Individuelle Lösung

A typical week (Seite 81)
13: Individuelle Lösungen

Unit 4 Check out (Seite 82-83)
1: Beispiellösungen:
1 We could go to the park. **2** Let's play video games. **3** I've got an idea. **4** I'm not sure.
5 Good idea! <u>oder:</u> Excellent plan!
2: 1 What **2** When <u>oder:</u> Where **3** How
4 Where **5** Who **6** How
3: 1 Harry's **2** Ava's **3** Harry and Lily's
4 Tarek's **5** Mr Hu's **6** Ava's family's
4: 1 no **2** no **3** no **4** yes
5: 1 On Mondays Jacinda goes to the science club. **2** On Tuesdays and Thursdays it's her turn to make dinner. **3** On Fridays Jacinda meets her dad. **4** On Saturdays Jacinda and her mum clean the house. **5** On Sundays they meet Jacinda's grandma or go to the park.
6: 1 Noah never makes breakfast on Sundays. **2** He sometimes cleans up after dinner. **3** He often takes Ollie for a walk and feeds him. **4** Noah always does the shopping for his grandma on Fridays.

Unit 5A
The best birthday (Seite 84)
1a: Individuelle Lösung
1b: 1 lots **2** chocolate **3** in the garden with his friends **4** because they are Hannah's favourite breakfast
1c+d: Individuelle Lösungen

Ava's birthday plans (seite 85)
2a: nine people
2b I: Ava's birthday – 4th June; Ava's guests – friends and family; what Ava wants to do first – go bowling; what dad says – pizza in the garden; Mum's ideas for the party – garden party, barbecue and pool; what they are planning in the end – garden party, barbecue, pool and selfie box

2b II: 1 4th June **2** friends and family **3** go bowling **4** pizza in the garden **5** garden party with barbecue **6** garden party, barbecue, pool, selfie box
2b III: Beispiellösung:
1 on the 4th of June **2** Grandma Edyta
3 five **4** go bowling **5** get pizza and sit in the garden **6** a garden party with a barbecue and setting up the pool **7** a garden party with a barbecue, the pool and a selfie box

Ava's garden party (Seite 86)
3a: 1 false **2** true **3** false **4** true **5** true **6** false
3a Challenge: 1 Joshua is drawing monsters. **3** Noah is buying some more balloons and birthday candles. **6** Ollie is jumping into the pool.
3b I-III: 1 Tarek and Ollie are wearing party hats. **2** Joshua and Aunt Hannah aren't dancing. **3** Ollie isn't eating birthday cake. **4** Ava and Noah aren't decorating the garden. **5** Ava is taking a selfie. **6** Grandpa isn't jumping into the pool. **7** Grandpa is kissing grandma. **8** Harry and Lily are singing a birthday song.

The months of the year (Seite 87)
4a: November / March / September / February / July / May / December / October / January / June / April / August
4b: 1 February **2** May **3** March and May
4 December, January, February
4b Challenge: Individuelle Lösung
4c: 1 22nd March **2** 14th December **3** 23rd July
4d: 1 21st January **2** 31st December **3** 1st August **4** 4th June **5** 15th November **6** 2nd May

All the family (Seite 88)
5a: waagerecht: grandmother, husband, sister, grandfather, uncle, mother, wife **senkrecht:** daughter, brother, son, aunt, father
5b: 1 grandmother **2** son **3** cousins
4 husband **5** partner **6** aunt

An invitation (Seite 88)
6/A-C: Individuelle Lösungen

Sound check (Seite 88)
7a+b: Individuelle Lösung

Practise reading: Tarek's birthday party (S. 89)
8a: Beispiellösung:
alien and space party, create your own costume, paint your face, do karaoke songs, eat astronaut ice cream, put up small lights, use glitter
8b: Beispiellösung:
you need: a great costume **activities:** do karaoke songs **food:** astronaut ice cream **decorations:** small lights, glitter

Party tips (Seite 89)
9: 1 Partycracker zu machen. **2** leere Toilettenpapierrollen. **3** kleinen lustigen Dingen. **4** auf der Webseite.

Happy birthday, Tarek! (Seite 90)
10a I: 1 Yes, he is. **2** Yes, they are. **3** No, she isn't. **4** No, it isn't.
10a II: 1 Is Tarek's uncle singing a birthday song? – Yes, he is. **2** What are the children eating? – Crisps and astronaut ice cream. **3** Is Tarek wearing a space suit? – No, he isn't. **4** Is Tarek's dad cleaning the living room? – No, he isn't.
10a III: 1 What is Tarek's uncle singing? – a birthday song oder: Happy birthday to you.
2 What are the children drinking? – lots of lemonade **3** Why can't Harry move his hands? – He is wearing a space suit. **4** Is the treasure hunt on the moon? – No, it isn't.
10b: astronaut ice cream – Astronauteneis-creme, space suit – Raumanzug, robot-alien – außerirdischer Roboter, treasure hunt – Schatzsuche, moon stones – Mondsteine
10c: Beispiellösung:
The children are having an aliens and space party. I can see Tarek, Ava, Noah and Lily. They

are wearing great costumes. Tarek is a space cowboy. Ava is wearing her blue hat. Lily is bringing something to eat. They are playing a game in the living room. There are nice decorations. Tarek is talking on the phone.

Planning a cool birthday party (Seite 91)
11: Individuelle Lösungen

Unit 5B
A day out in Brighton (Seite 92)
1a+b: Individuelle Lösungen
1b Challenge: Individuelle Lösung

Last year in Brighton (Seite 92)
2 I: 1 That was a really crazy seagull. **2** It was very hungry! **3** Weren't you scared of the seagull? **4** Oh yes, we were.
2 II: 1 This was at the pier. **2** Was that at Brighton beach, too? **3** That was a really crazy seagull. **4** Weren't you scared of the seagull?
2 III: 1 It was my first time. **2** Harry wasn't very good at it. **3** That was a really crazy seagull. **4** Weren't you scared of the seagull? **5** Was that at Brighton beach, too? **6** Harry and I were there with some friends.

What about the weather? (Seite 93)
3 I: Beispiellösung:
windy, rainy – sunny, warm – rainy, cold
3 II: Beispiellösung:
On Friday the weather is windy, cold, cloudy and rainy. On Saturday it is windy and sunny, cloudy and warm. On Sunday the weather is rainy, cold and windy. I like the weather on Friday because I like windy days.
3 III: Individuelle Lösung
3 Challenge: Individuelle Lösung

Going to Brighton (Seite 93-94)
4a: Harry, Lily, Ava, Tarek, Harry and Lily's mum
4b: 1 false **2** true **3** true **4** false **5** false **6** false
4b Challenge: 1 Lily and Harry want to show Ava and Tarek the beach in Brighton. Noah can't come. **4** They want to go on Saturday. **5** They book tickets for the train at nine o'clock. **6** Lily and Harry's mum is coming, too.

A day in Brighton (Seite 94)
5 I: 1 Today was an exciting day! **2** I was at the beach but there weren't any people there. **3** So there was no food around. **4** Then there were some children on the beach with a yummy sandwich. **5** And swoosh! – I wasn't hungry anymore. **6** I was a happy seagull with a yummy sandwich!
5 II: Beispiellösung:
We were at Brighton beach today. It was great! There were some cool fatbikes for us. Some of the tricks were really hard. My friend and I were very good at it. It was so much fun!
5 III: Individuelle Lösung

They weren't in Brighton (Seite 95)
6: 1 Harry wasn't at the bike park, he was at the beach. **2** Lily wasn't in the kitchen, she was in the lab. **3** Ava wasn't at school, she was at home. **4** Double and Trouble weren't in the cage, they were in the garden. **5** Tarek wasn't at the gym, he was at the cafeteria. **6** Mr Hu wasn't at the shop, he was at the park.

The video message (Seite 95)
7a: 1 Brighton Palace Pier **2** Upside Down House **3** Royal Pavilion **4** i360 tower **5** the Lanes
7b: Individuelle Lösung
7b Challenge: 1 You can see an amusement park and you can eat fish and chips. <u>oder:</u> amusement park, eat fish and chips **2** It is special because everything is upside down. <u>oder:</u> everything is upside down **3** It is more than 200 years old. <u>oder:</u> more than 200 years **4** You can buy silly things. <u>oder:</u> silly things **5** The Lanes are small

streets. <u>oder:</u> small streets

Noah's message to his friends (Seite 96)
8 I: video pier tower souvenir
8 II: Beispiellösung:
1 Hi guys, what a cool video! **2** The i360 and the Royal Pavilion are my favourite things. **3** Now I really want to go to Brighton, too! **4** Can you please bring me a Brighton Rock candy stick as a souvenir? **5** See you soon, Noah
8 III: Individuelle Lösung

Rules at the pier (Seite 96)
9: Beispiellösung:
1 Man darf nicht vom Pier springen. **2** Man darf am Pier nicht fischen. **3** Man darf hier nicht schwimmen. **4** Man darf die Möwen nicht füttern. **5** Man muss aufpassen, weil hier Fatbikes und Skater unterwegs sind.

Seaside towns (Seite 96)
10/A+B: Individuelle Lösungen
10/C: Beispiellösung:
fish and chips with vinegar, candy sticks, ice cream, mussels, shellfish

Practise reading: Shopping in Brighton (Seite 97)
11a-c: Individuelle Lösungen

Mum's day out (Seite 98)
12a: Beispiellösung:
1 I was at my friend Mulan's house. **2** She has a new baby, Liu. **3** He is so cute. **4** We were at the beach. **5** It was sunny and warm there. **6** Then we had tea in the garden. **7** I like Mulan a lot. **8** It was so nice to see her again.
12b: **1** No, she wasn't. **2** Yes, they were. **3** No, they weren't. **4** No, she wasn't. **5** Yes, he was. **6** Yes, they were. **7** No, he wasn't. **8** Yes, she was.

Writing a postcard (Seite 99)
13: Individuelle Lösungen

Unit 5 Check out (Seite 100-101)
1: Joshua is listening to music. Noah is brushing his teeth. Ava is lying on her bed. Mr Kogan is doing yoga. Mrs Kogan is reading a book. Ollie is playing with his ball.
2: Beispiellösung:
Hoo is Mee's brother. Bee is Moo's aunt. Woo and Wee are cousins. Hoo and Bee are husband and wife. Moo's birthday is on the twenty-first of November. Hoo's birthday is on the sixth of June. Bee's birthday is on the third of September.
3: Beispiellösung:
1 im Garten oder hinter dem Haus **2** für alle, die im Sommer Geburtstag haben **3** gute Filme, einen Computer, eine Leinwand, Stühle oder Matratzen, Getränke, jede Menge Popcorn und Snacks **4** sich wie die eigene Lieblingsfigur aus einem Film zu verkleiden
4: **1** Tarek wasn't at the park, he was at the ice rink. **2** Lily wasn't at Ava's place, she was at Portobello Road Market with her mums. **3** Harry wasn't in town with his friends, he was at school with the school band. **4** Joshua wasn't at home, he was at the playground with his dad.
5: **1** um 9:15 Uhr **2** auf der linken Seite **3** Sie sollen an ihre Sachen denken und ihre Jacken, Hüte, Taschen und Schirme nicht vergessen.
6: Beispiellösung:
1 Hello. Can I help you? **2** Hello. Have you got vegetarian sausages? **3** Yes, we do. They are in the fridge next to the cheese. **4** Thank you. Could I have chocolate biscuits, too? **5** Yes, of course, here you are. That's six pounds and 50 pence. **6** Here you are. Ten pounds. **7** That's three pounds and fifty pence change. **8** Thank you, have a nice day. **9** Thank you, you too. Goodbye.

Great places in your area TARGET TASK SUPPORT

11 wordbank: places p. 152, free time p. 157

1 Do you remember the question words? Match the English and the German words.

what	wie
where	wann
when	was
how	wie viel
how much	wo

2 Write down the best places for children in your area. What can you do there?

Ponyhof "Wäldchen": you can ride cute little ponies

3 Which place is your favourite?

4 What do you know about your favourite place? What can you find out? Make notes.

What is it? *It is a*

Where is it? *It is in*

When is it open? *It is open* *from* *to*

How much is it? *It is €* *for children and €* *for*

What can you do there? *You can*

What is good or special about it? *It is*

There are

Tipp: Einen Steckbrief erstellen und korrigieren

1 Du hast dich für einen interessanten Ort entschieden? Dann suche jetzt nach Informationen. Frage deine Freunde oder deine Eltern. Vielleicht habt ihr Prospekte zu Hause? Suche auch mal im Internet.
2 Notiere alles, was du wichtig und interessant findest.
3 Welche Informationen sind auch für andere Kinder wichtig, die etwas über den Ort erfahren wollen? Das sind die Informationen, die du für deinen Steckbrief brauchst. Notiere sie auf Englisch.
4 Sieh nach, ob du die Informationen auch richtig notiert hast.
5 Prüfe im Wörterbuch, ob du alles richtig geschrieben hast.

Die Check out-Seiten helfen dir einzuschätzen, was du schon gut kannst und was du noch üben solltest.
Löse die Aufgaben auf dieser Doppelseite und male die Kreise wie bei einer Ampel rot, gelb oder grün aus.

Rot: Das kann ich noch nicht.

Gelb: Das fällt mir noch schwer.

Grün: Das kann ich gut.

1 Kannst du ausdrücken, was jemand hat oder nicht hat?
2 Kannst du verstehen, was jemand über sich selbst erzählt?
3 Kannst du etwas über dich erzählen?
4 Kannst du einen kurzen Text über einen Ort verstehen?
5 Kannst du Fragen zu Orten stellen und beantworten?
6 Kannst du einen Ort in deiner Nachbarschaft beschreiben?

1

Write down what the children have got ✓ and haven't got X.

1 ______________________
2 ______________________
3 ______________________
4 ______________________
5 ______________________
6 ______________________

	Arsenal poster	sister	cat
Alisha	✓	X	✓
Roy and Arlo	X	✓	X

Ich kann ausdrücken, was jemand hat oder nicht hat. ◯

2 audio 1/24

Listen to Lewis. Fill in the information about him.

name: ______________________
lives in: ______________________
family: ______________________
pet: ______________________
likes: ______________________
hates: ______________________
hobbies: ______________________
favourite things: ______________________

Ich kann verstehen, was jemand über sich selbst erzählt. ◯

3

You are Ella or Paul. Talk about yourself. Record it.

You can say:

Hi, I'm Ella / Paul. I'm from
I live with
I've got
I like
My

Ella / Paul
* Oxford (England)
* parents, a brother
* two hamsters, three cats
* ☺ films about animals, vanilla pudding
* hobbies: singing, reading
* favourite things: fantasy books, tablet

Ich kann etwas über mich erzählen. ◯

4

Read about Lisa's neighbourhood. Then tick ✓ true or false.

My neighbourhood is very nice and green. There are a lot of old houses with gardens. Near my house there is a place for children. You can play there, paint, listen to music and do a lot of other things. It is open from Monday to Friday. My friends and I really like it. The swimming pool is another great place in my neighbourhood. It is big and new. It is an indoor pool so you can go there in the summer and in the winter. There is a small park in my neighbourhood, too. My friends and I play ball games in the park.

	true	false
1 There are a lot of new houses in Lisa's neighbourhood.	☐	☐
2 There is a place for parents near Lisa's house.	☐	☐
3 The swimming pool is new.	☐	☐
4 There is a small park in Lisa's neighbourhood.	☐	☐
5 Lisa and her friends relax in the park.	☐	☐

Ich kann einen kurzen Text über einen Ort verstehen. ◯

5

John is new in Lisa's neighbourhood. Write down his questions and Lisa's answers.

	John's questions		Lisa's answers
cinema?	*Is there*	+	
museums?		–	
market?		–	
cafés?		+	

Ich kann Fragen zu Orten stellen und beantworten. ◯

6

Write a short text for Aidan about a place in his neighbourhood.

big playground · in a park · go skateboarding with my friends · open daily · favourite place · cool

There is ______________________ *in my neighbourhood. It* ______________________

Ich kann einen Ort in meiner Nachbarschaft beschreiben. ◯

Wenn du noch mehr üben möchtest, gehe zu Practise more - Unit 1. DIGITAL+

Pack your schoolbag!

1a

Fill in the crossword.

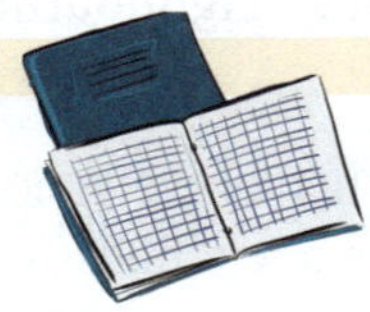

1b

Work with a partner. Talk about your schoolbags.

You can ask:
Have you got exercise books in your schoolbag?
Have you got a pencil case in your schoolbag?
Have you got …

You can answer:
Yes, I have.
No, I haven't.

School things in Tarek's room

2a

audio 1/26, skill: listening p. 141

Listen to Tarek. Number the school things in the order you hear them.

☐ schoolbag ☐ pencil case ☐ exercise books ☐ calculator ☐ folders

☐ pencil sharpener ☐ pens ☐ eraser ☐ pencils ☐ ruler

2b CHOOSE YOUR LEVEL

Listen to Tarek again.

I **Write down the things that are in Tarek's schoolbag.**

_ _ _ _ _ _ _   _ _ _ _ _ _ _ _   _ _ _ _ _

II **Write down the things Tarek puts in his pencil case.**

III **Write down the things that are in Tarek's schoolbag, the things he puts in his pencil case and the things Dad gives to Tarek.**

Check the teacher's bag

3 wordbank: school p. 154

What can you see? Write down the school things.

I can see

There is

There are

Challenge: **Write down the things that are not school things.**

Practise reading

Tipp 3
Wenn es zu einem Text Bilder gibt, sieh sie dir an. Sie können dir Hinweise auf den Inhalt des Textes geben.

Assembly

4a

Look at the picture. What can you see? Who is there? Where are the people? Make notes in German or English.

___

___

___

___

4b audio 1/27

Read the text. Underline the information from your notes in 4a.

Headteacher: Good morning, boys and girls! Welcome to Holland Park School. My name is Mr Walker and I am your headteacher. Today is an exciting day – but don't be nervous! Let me tell you a bit about your new school. Assembly is every morning at twenty to nine. We all meet here for important information. Always be on time, please. After assembly you go to registration. Registration is every morning at nine o'clock. Lunch is at half past twelve and there are a lot of activities in the afternoon. Look at the noticeboard for information. I hope you have a good first day and a great year at Holland Park School! If you have any problems, come and see me in my office. Now it's time to meet your new class. We start with class …

4c

Tick ✓ the correct sentence ending.

1 The headteacher is talking about …
- ☐ the new school.
- ☐ the problems at school.

2 You can find information …
- ☐ at the headteacher's office.
- ☐ at the noticeboard.

PRACTISE READING

Hat **Tipp 3** dir geholfen, den Text zu verstehen? ◯ ja ◯ teilweise ◯ nein

Eat your spaghetti!

5 CHOOSE YOUR LEVEL grammar: imperatives p. 170

Match the sentences in the box and the pictures.

I Write four sentences.
II Write seven sentences.
III Write ten sentences.

~~Don't talk.~~ · Listen to the song. · Open your pencil cases. · Look at my new shoes. · Don't shout at me. · Don't eat here. · Open the door, please. · Don't play with the ball here. · Eat your spaghetti. · Look at my homework. · Don't run here. · Take out your pens.

1 Don't talk.
2 ______
3 ______

1 ______
2 ______
3 ______

1 ______
2 ______
3 ______

1 ______
2 ______
3 ______

Sound check

6 audio 1/28

Learn to say the letter 'u'.
Listen to the words and repeat them.
Circle the words that sound like 'mum'.

mum · bus · uniform · June · much · put · funny · number · blue · but · museum · club

LANGUAGE HELP am *und* pm

am und *pm*: diese Abkürzungen findet man häufig an Uhrzeiten und auf Uhren mit digitaler 12-Stunden Anzeige.
am ist von 12h nachts bis 12h mittags, *pm* ist von 12h mittags bis 12h nachts.

Beispiel: *8am* = 8h morgens, *8pm* = 20h abends. Merke dir die Eselsbrücke: *am* = <u>a</u>m <u>M</u>orgen.

What's the time?

7a wordbank: time p. 155, numbers p. 231

Draw the times on the clocks.

1 [:]
It's four o'clock.

2 [:]
It's eleven o'clock.

3 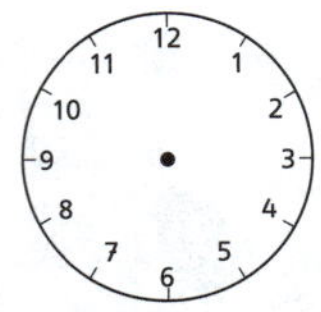
It's half past eight.

4 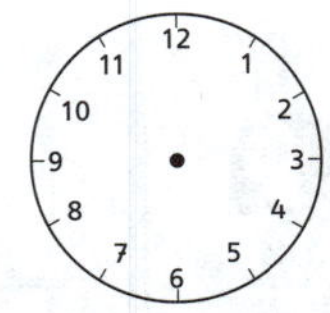
It's quarter past ten.

7b audio 1/29

Listen. Draw the times on the clocks.

1 [:]

2 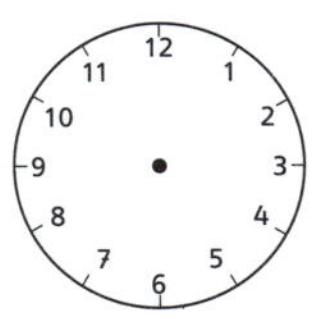

3 [:]

4 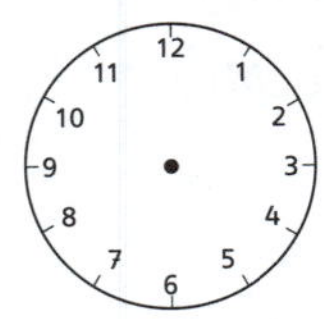

7c

Write down the times under the clocks.

1 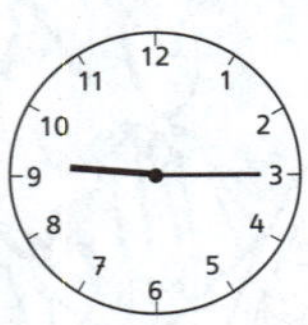

______

2 04:30

______

3 18:40

______

4 03:10

______

7d

Draw times on the clocks. Then write down the times under the clocks. Check with a partner.

1 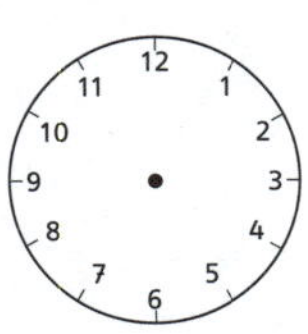

______

2 [:]

______

3 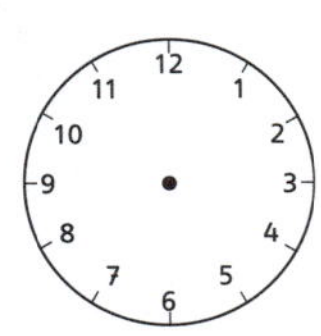

______

4 [:]

______

7e skill: mediation p. 145

Wie sagt man die Uhrzeit auf Englisch und auf Deutsch oder in einer anderen Sprache, die du kennst? Beispiele: 9.45, 11.30. Gibt es Unterschiede? Mach dir Notizen. Erzähle davon in der Klasse.

______

School subjects

8a

Find the words for school subjects in the word snake.

8b wordbank: school p. 154

Which subjects do you like? Which don't you like? Write them down. Start with your favourite subject.

8c

Write about your subjects.

My favourite subject is ____________________ *, because[1] I like* ____________________

I like ____

I don't like ____________________ *, because* ____________________

____

____

1 **because** – weil

Spelling fun

9 CHOOSE YOUR TASK

A **Choose a letter. Write down all the words you know that start with that letter.** *t: take, task, time, …*

B **Work with a partner. Spell your favourite words. Take turns.**

C **Write your timetable in English. Check the spelling of the words in your dictionary.**

LANGUAGE HELP *der unbestimmte Artikel* TB p.171

Achte auf die Aussprache! Wenn das Wort nach einem unbestimmten Artikel mit einem Vokallaut beginnt, benutzt man nicht *a*, sondern *an*. Beispiel: *a pen* aber *an eraser*

A or *an*?

10a grammar: article p. 171

Add a or an.

____ computer ____ eraser ____ ruler ____ orange ball ____ activity

____ pencil ____ open book ____ folder ____ English teacher ____ office

10b audio 1/36

Listen and check your articles. Repeat the words.

Classroom questions

11

Unscramble the questions. Write them down.

1 page – What – please? ______________________

2 pencil sharpener? – Where – your – is ______________________

3 spell – please? – Can – you – calculator ______________________

4 is – homework – in – What – German? ______________________

5 borrow – please? – Can – ruler – I – a ______________________

More spelling

12a audio 1/38

Listen and write down the words.

1 __ __ __ 2 __ __ __ __ __ 3 __ __ __ __

4 __ __ __ __ __ 5 __ __ __ __ 6 __ __ __ __ 7 __ __ __

12b audio 1/39

Write down the plural of the words. Then listen to the plural words and repeat them.

1 __ __ __ __ __ 2 __ __ __ __ __ __ __ __ 3 __ __ __ __ __ __

4 __ __ __ __ __ __ __ 5 __ __ __ __ 6 __ __ __ __ __ 7 __ __ __

A classroom board game TARGET TASK SUPPORT

13 wordbank: school p. 154, grammar: imperatives p. 170

1 Collect words and phrases in the boxes.

subjects	things in the classroom
maths *PE*	*desk*

school things	difficult words
folder	*registration*

2 Write more tasks or questions for the challenge cards.

Name two subjects you have on Mondays.	*Name* ______
Point at the bin!	*Point at* ______
Say "red card, blue card" fast for 20 seconds.	*Say* ______
What time does school start on Fridays?	*What time* ______
Who lives in a small blue house?	*Who* ______
Who has got two rabbits?	*Who has got* ______

3 Match the English and the German phrases.

1 Take a card.	Würfle noch einmal.
2 Read the card out loud.	Gehe drei Felder zurück.
3 It's your turn.	Gehe zwei Felder vor.
4 Roll the dice.	Du bist dran.
5 Roll again.	Nimm eine Karte.
6 Miss a turn.	Fang von vorne an.
7 Go back three steps.	Du musst aussetzen.
8 Go two steps forward.	Würfle.
9 Start again.	Lies die Karte vor.

Tipp: **Bevor du das Spiel spielst, höre dir die englischen Sätze an und sprich sie nach.** audio 1/40

Practise reading

Tipp 4

Wenn du genaue Informationen aus einem Text herauslesen willst, kannst du ihn nach und nach durchgehen. Folgende Fragen können dir helfen:

What? (Was?) Who? (Wer?)
When? (Wann?) Where? (Wo?)

What's on at Holland Park School?

1a

Look at the poster and read the questions.

What is the name of the club? → **Drama club**

Be a star at the drama club!
When: Mondays, 4:00pm – 6:00pm ← When does it take place?
Where: assembly hall ← Where does it take place?
Who: everybody is welcome ← Who can come?
For more information talk to Mrs Baker.

1b audio 1/41

Look at the posters. Find the information for the question words. Underline the information in the same colour.

Cooking club
Do you like cooking?
Then join our cooking club!
Who: all students are welcome!
Where: school kitchen
When: Tuesdays, 4:15pm – 5:45pm

What?
When?
Where?
Who?

Football team
The football team needs you!
We practise at the gym on Wednesdays from 4:00pm – 5:30pm.
We play matches on Saturdays.

PRACTISE READING

Hat **Tipp 4** dir geholfen, den Text zu verstehen? ◯ ja ◯ teilweise ◯ nein

A club for Nina and Freddie

2 audio 1/42

Listen to the children. Tick ✓ the club they choose.

☐ science club ☐ drama club ☐ cooking club

Challenge: Which club do you like? Say why. Write it in your exercise book.

Clubs at Holland Park School

3a CHOOSE YOUR LEVEL grammar: simple present p. 173

Look at the posters in TB1 again.

Answer three questions or more.
Answer five questions or more.
Answer the questions.

1 What can you do at the book club? *read one new book every month*
2 Where does the cooking club take place? ______
3 When does the football team play matches? ______
4 Who can come to the drama club? ______
5 Where does the science club meet? ______
6 What do you have to bring to the school band? ______
7 Who can you talk to about the drama club? ______
8 When does the school band meet? ______

3b grammar: simple present p. 173

Read the posters in TB1 again. Write down five sentences in your exercise book.

1 The book club	practises	every month.
2 The football team	reads one new book	on Saturdays.
3 The school band	does exciting experiments	every Friday.
4 The science club	plays matches	on Thursdays.
5 The football team	meets with instruments	every Wednesday.

The days of the week

4 wordbank: time p. 155

Answer the questions.

1 Which day comes after Saturday? ______
2 Which day has nine letters? ______
3 Which two days have eight letters? ______
4 Which day comes before Tuesday? ______
5 Which day is the first in the alphabet? ______
6 Which two days start with the letter T? ______

Challenge: Write more questions like this for a partner in your exercise book.

That doesn't sound bad

5a CHOOSE YOUR LEVEL audio 1/43, grammar: simple present p. 173

Listen to Lily and Ava again.

I Complete the sentences with verbs from the box.

sounds · goes · says · says

1 Noah ______________ the science club is great.
2 Noah ______________ they do a lot of experiments.
3 That ______________ great!
4 Noah ______________ to lunch before his lunchtime clubs.

II Complete the sentences with verbs from the box.

likes · meet · says · try · says · goes

1 Noah ______________ the science club is great.
2 Noah ______________ they do a lot of experiments.
3 Ava ______________ the book club.
4 They ______________ today at lunchtime.
5 Noah ______________ to lunch before his lunchtime clubs.
6 Lily and Ava ______________ the book club.

III Complete the sentences with verbs from the box.

says · doesn't sound · likes · doesn't like · try · goes · meet · doesn't play

1 Lily ________________________ an instrument.
2 She ________________________ team sports.
3 Noah ________________________ the science club is great.
4 That ________________________ bad.
5 Ava ________________________ the book club.
6 They ________________________ today at lunchtime.
7 Noah ________________________ to lunch before his lunchtime clubs.
8 Lily and Ava ________________________ the book club.

5b

Look at TB1a again. Which school clubs do you like?

1 I like ________________________________
2 I don't like ________________________________
3 I think ________________________________ is great.
4 ________________________________ sounds great!
5 I don't want to try ________________________________
6 ________________________________ doesn't sound bad.

More school clubs

6 CHOOSE YOUR TASK

A **Read the poster and fill in the table.**

What?	
Who can come?	
When?	
Where?	
Who is the teacher?	

Computer club

- Do you like computers? Our new school computers are here.
- We have 10 free places for boys and girls.
- We meet on Tuesdays from 4pm to 5pm in the computer room.
- Talk to Ms Jameson and join our new computer club!

B **Make a list of all the school clubs you know.**

C **Write about your dream school club.**

Ava and Lily at school

7

Find the sentences in the word snakes. Write them in your exercise book.

1 Lilydoesn'tliketeamsports.

2 Noahsaysthescienceclubisgreat.

3 Atthescienceclubtheydoexperiments.

4 Thescienceclubdoesn'tsoundbad.

5 Lunchbeforethebookclubisn'taproblem.

6 Avadoesn'tgotothescienceclub.

7 Lilylikesapplepiealot.

8 Thegirlswanttotrythebookclub.

Sound check

8a audio 1/44

Listen to the 's' sounds that the bee and the snake make. Listen again and make the sounds.

zzz /z/

sss /s/

8b audio 1/45

Listen and repeat the verbs.

says · likes · sounds · practises · tries · thinks · goes · meets · looks · wants · plays · reads

Tarek and his uncle

9 grammar: simple present p. 173

Read TB7b again. Complete the answers.

1 Where does Tarek do experiments? Tarek ______________ experiments at the science lab.

2 Where does Tarek go on Tuesdays? He ______________ to the cooking club on Tuesdays.

3 What does Mr Patel teach? Mr Patel ______________ English and music.

4 Where does Tarek play football? Tarek ______________ football at the sports ground.

5 Where does Tarek practise when it rains? When it rains he ______________ at the gym.

All about school

10a

Match the words and the definitions[1].

1 **definition** – Erklärung, Definition

break · assembly · school uniform · school club · house · registration

1 The teacher reads out the names of the children to check who is there.
____

2 In the afternoon students can do fun courses at school or learn about something special.
____

3 Everyone meets in a big hall in the morning.
____

4 Time at school when the students can play, eat and drink.
____

5 A group of students – each group has its own colour and a name. They play matches against each other.
____

6 The clothes that students of one school wear, usually with the school logo on them.
____

10b CHOOSE YOUR LEVEL skill: mediation p. 145

Explain the definitions in German. Take notes.

I Explain definitions 1 and 2.

II Explain definitions 1, 2, 3 and 4.

III Explain the definitions.

____

____

____

____

____

____

10c wordbank: clothes p. 153

What do Ava and her friends wear at school? Label the clothes.

1 

grey pullover

2 

3 

4 

5 

6 

7 

8 

A video chat with friends

11 CHOOSE YOUR LEVEL audio 1/47

Listen to Lily and her friends in TB8b again.

I Complete the answers with words from the box.

they · she · they · he · they

1 Does Lily talk to her friends in London? No, ________ doesn't.
2 Do Ellen and Jonah miss Lily? Yes, ________ do.
3 Does Harry still play the guitar? Yes, ________ does.
4 Do Lily and Harry wear a school uniform? Yes, ________ do.
5 Do Ellen and Jonah wear a black uniform? No, ________ don't.

II Match the questions and the answers.

1 Does Lily think London is cool? — Yes, they do.
2 Does Ellen like school without Lily? — No, they don't.
3 Does Harry play in a band? — Yes, she does.
4 Do Ellen and Jonah wear a red uniform? — No, she doesn't.
5 Do they like their uniform? — Yes, he does.

III Answer the questions.

1 Does Lily have a video chat with friends in London? ________
2 Does Ellen still go to drama club? ________
3 Do Jonah and Ellen wear a red school uniform? ________
4 Does Lily wear a black skirt to school? ________
5 Do Harry and Lily wear a black shirt to school? ________

The rooms at school

12a

Look at the pictures. Match the activities in the box and the pictures.

learn together · play instruments · have lunch · do experiments · read books · ~~do sports~~ · learn to cook · meet for assembly

1 gym

do sports

2 assembly hall

3 school kitchen

4 music room

5 classroom

6 science lab

7 library

8 cafeteria

12b

Write six sentences in your exercise book.

1 Tarek	meets	in the gym.
2 Ava	do sports	in the school kitchen.
3 Noah and Lily	learns to cook	in the classroom.
4 The students	do experiments	in the assembly hall.
5 The class	meet for assembly	in the library.
6 The students	reads books	in the science lab.

Welcome to our school

13 video 8

Watch the video clip in TB14a again. Tick ✓ the correct answers.

1 When is the library not open?	☐ before school	☐ break times	☐ after school
2 What do they not have in the sports hall?	☐ assembly	☐ PE	☐ lunch
3 What is not part of the school uniform?	☐ a tie	☐ a shirt	☐ a T-shirt

Our school TARGET TASK SUPPORT

14 wordbank: school p. 154, skills: presentations p. 146

Complete the sentences with information about your school. You can use the words in brackets ( ).

Our school is ____________________

(really big, nice, very old)

The ____________________ *(best, special)* thing about our school is

____

The teachers at our school are ____________________

(friendly, strict, helpful)

We all really like ____________________

(our form teacher, Mrs …, Mr …)

There ____________________ *(are, aren't)* many clubs after school.

There is ____________________

and ____________________

I go to ____________________

These are the rooms in our school:

We have ____________ *(many, 22)* classrooms.

There are ____________________

and a ____________________

We also have a ____________________

(library, music room)

Our classroom is ____________________

____

These are the places outdoors:

Behind the school there is ____________________

Next to the school is our ____________________

We also have got a ____________________

____

(basketball court, garden)

Tipp: So kannst du eine Gruppenpräsentation moderieren

Ein Schüler / eine Schülerin kann alleine moderieren oder sich mit anderen abwechseln.
Am Anfang erzählst du, was präsentiert wird. Dann stellst du den ersten Redebeitrag vor.

- *Today we want to present information about our school.*
- *First Bijan presents the rooms in our school in a slide show.*

Bedanke dich bei jedem Redner / jeder Rednerin und sage, was als Nächstes kommt.

- *Thank you Bijan, that was interesting.*
- *This is Karoline with a video about the places outdoors.*
- *That was great, Karoline. Thank you.*
- *Next are Amra and Georg with a presentation about our teachers.*
- *Very good, Amra and Georg, thank you.*

Am Ende bedankst du dich beim Publikum.

- *Thank you for listening. I hope it was interesting.*

Die Check out-Seiten helfen dir einzuschätzen, was du schon gut kannst und was du noch üben solltest.
Löse die Aufgaben auf dieser Doppelseite und male die Kreise wie auf Seite 28 rot, gelb oder grün aus.

1. Kannst du jemanden auffordern, etwas zu tun oder nicht zu tun?
2. Kannst du Dinge in deiner Schultasche und in deinem Klassenzimmer benennen?
3. Kannst du die Uhrzeit auf Englisch nennen?
4. Kannst du darüber berichten, was regelmäßig stattfindet oder was jemand regelmäßig tut?
5. Kannst du verstehen, was jemand über den Schulalltag berichtet?
6. Kannst du jemandem Fragen zur Schule stellen?

1

What does Mr Patel tell his class? Write sentences.

\+ read a lot of books · do your homework · have fun at school

– use your phone in class · be late for the lesson · forget your books

Ich kann jemanden auffordern, etwas zu tun oder nicht zu tun.

2

Complete the sentences.

1 You put your pens, your pencils and your eraser in your ____________ ____________

2 You do your homework in your ____________ ____________

3 Our teachers write on the ____________

4 There are ____________ with a lot of books in our classroom.

5 My friend and I sit at the same ____________

6 In the evening I pack my ____________ for the next day.

Ich kann die Dinge in meiner Schultasche und in meinem Klassenzimmer benennen.

3

Match the clocks and the times. Draw lines. Then point to the clocks and say the times.

1 

2 10:15

3 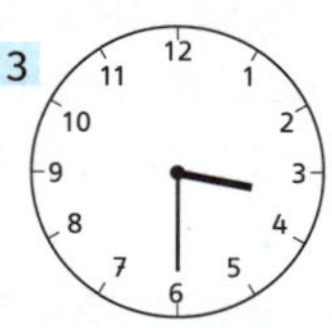

4 09:45

5 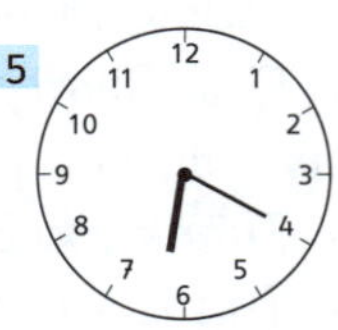

It's quarter past ten.	It's twenty past six.	It's quarter to ten.	It's eight o'clock.	It's half past three.

Ich kann die Uhrzeit auf Englisch nennen.

4

What do the people do when? Write about their activities.

Tarek's uncle Sami
go / fitness class / Wednesdays
meet / friends / weekend

Jonah and Ellen
practise / school band / Tuesdays
go / library / Thursday afternoons

Ich kann darüber berichten, was regelmäßig stattfindet oder was jemand regelmäßig tut.

5 audio 1/49

Listen to Badu talking about his school day. Complete the sentences.

1 Assembly is at ______ every morning.
2 ______ is at seven fifty.
3 After that we have ______.
4 Lunch is from ______ to ______.
5 Then we have another ______.
6 On Thursday afternoons I go to ______.

Ich kann verstehen, was jemand über den Schulalltag berichtet.

6

You meet a British student. What can you ask him or her? Unscramble the questions.

1 do you · uniform · wear · a school · ? ______
2 teachers · your · do you · like · ? ______
3 school · do you · when · start · in the morning · ? ______
4 your · what · subject · is · favourite · ? ______
5 school · go · do you · club · to a · ? ______

Ich kann jemandem Fragen zur Schule stellen.

Wenn du noch mehr üben möchtest, gehe zu Practise more - Unit 2. DIGITAL+

Breakfast with Ava's family

1a

Read TB1 again. Fill in the lists.

cold food	hot food	drinks	things to set the table

Challenge: **Add more breakfast words to the lists.**

1b

Read TB1 again. Tick ✓ true or false.

	true	false
1 They need bacon, eggs and sausages.	☐	☐
2 Mum likes vegetarian sausages.	☐	☐
3 They don't need cereal.	☐	☐
4 Ava's dad sets the table.	☐	☐
5 Joshua puts the fruit on the table.	☐	☐
6 Noah always helps.	☐	☐

Challenge: **Correct the false sentences in your exercise book.**

1c

grammar: simple present questions p. 174

Match the questions and answers. Draw lines.

1 Is the family breakfast on Saturday?	No, she doesn't.
2 Does Ava's mum eat vegetarian sausages?	Yes, they do.
3 Do the children like tomatoes?	Yes, he is.
4 Do they need plates and cups?	Yes, it is.
5 Are all the children at the table?	No, they don't.
6 Is Noah always late for breakfast?	No, they aren't.

Different breakfasts

2 CHOOSE YOUR LEVEL wordbank: food p. 156

I **What does Ava's family have for breakfast? What does your family have for breakfast? Write the things that are the same in the middle.**

Ava's family | the same | my family

II **Write about Ava's breakfast and your breakfast. What is the same? What is different?**

Ava's family has ____________________ for breakfast.

My family has ____________________, too.

We don't have ____________________ for breakfast.

We always eat ____________________

Sometimes we ____________________

III **Write about Ava's breakfast and your breakfast in your exercise book. What is the same? What is different?**

What time is it?

3 audio 1/51, wordbank: time p. 155

Look at the clocks. Listen and number the clocks in the correct order.

☐ 11:40 ☐ 02:00 ☐ 05:30 1 02:45 ☐ 10:15 ☐ 15:20 ☐ 08:25 ☐ 13:50

Spot the difference

4a audio 1/52, wordbank: food p. 156

Look at picture 1. Listen, point and repeat the words.

1

2

4b wordbank: food p. 156

Write down what is not in picture 2.

4c CHOOSE YOUR LEVEL

Look at picture 1 again and make notes. Talk about it and record yourself. Edit your recording.
Talk about the picture for 30 seconds. Talk for 40 seconds. Talk for one minute.

Full English breakfast

5 skill: mediation p. 145

Du bist mit deiner Familie in London. Deine Eltern wollen ein traditionelles englisches Frühstück probieren. Schau dir die beiden Anzeigen an und beantworte ihre Fragen auf Deutsch.

Diana's café

This family-friendly café is in the city centre, a 3-minute walk from Kings Cross underground station. They offer traditional food and people love the full English breakfast with bacon, sausages, eggs, baked beans and grilled tomatoes. Some say the fresh orange juice is the best in London. They also offer a variety of coffee specialities. It's not cheap, but it's worth the money. Open daily from 6am – 1pm.

Lucky Lunch

Not far from Holland Park, Lucky Lunch is a new café that offers great food for a good price. Their breakfast special is homemade pancakes and fresh fruit. But, you can also order the traditional English breakfast and they have a vegetarian option, too. You can enjoy your food inside or in a small garden outside. Open from 7am – 3pm. Closed on Mondays.

1 In welchem Café gibt es denn das traditionelle englische Frühstück?
2 Wie kommen wir am einfachsten zu den Cafés? Wo sind sie in London?
3 Wird etwas darüber gesagt, was das englische Frühstück beinhaltet?
4 Papa ist doch Vegetarier. Gibt es etwas für ihn?
5 Sind die Cafés teuer?
6 Was wird über Spezialitäten gesagt?
7 Bei Diana's Café steht etwas über Orangensaft. Was wird denn gesagt?
8 Was ist mit den Öffnungszeiten? Wir möchten am Montag gehen. Ist das möglich?

Sound check

6 audio 1/53

Listen to the words and repeat them.
What do you notice about the letter 's'?
Does it sound like the bee /z/ or like the snake /s/?

song · sun · sing · someone · selfie · say · sock · see · sister · sorry · son · same · so

A breakfast survey

7 CHOOSE YOUR LEVEL audio 1/54, skill: listening p. 141

Listen to Mathilda, Nick and Kerim. What do they say about breakfast at the weekend?

I Underline the correct words and phrases.

Mathilda: She eats at her **grandparents' / parents'** café. Her favourite is an egg and **avocado / sausage** sandwich. Her brother likes a **sweet / big** breakfast.
Nick: He normally just eats **an egg / two eggs** and some toast. His **dad / mum** always says: "That is not enough. Eat some fruit, have some yoghurt." His parents **don't like / like** a big breakfast at the weekend. But Nick is not hungry in the morning.
Kerim: His **grandpa / grandma** always makes a full English breakfast for the family. They have everything: sausages, bacon, eggs, baked beans, tomatoes, toast and **orange juice / oranges.** They talk about their week and make plans for the next **week / weekend**. It's so much fun.

II Correct the sentences in your exercise book.

1 Mathilda and her brother eat breakfast at home.
2 They eat the same things for breakfast.
3 Nick normally eats breakfast on a bicycle tour.
4 He eats some fruit, yoghurt and porridge.
5 Kerim's parents make breakfast for the family.
6 He is not hungry in the morning and only drinks some orange juice.

III Answer the questions in your exercise book.

1 Who has a favourite breakfast and what is it?
2 Who is not hungry in the morning?
3 Who eats toast for breakfast?
4 Why does Nick's mum tell him to eat some fruit or yoghurt?
5 Who is there for breakfast at Kerim's house?
6 What do they talk about?

Challenge: What about you? What do you eat for breakfast at the weekend? Write about it in your exercise book or make a recording.

Bathroom words

8

Find the bathroom words in the word snake.

SHOWER|CLEANSTYLETEETHWASHBRUSHEARSBATHROOMCOMBHAIRSMELLY

Noah in the bathroom

9a grammar: word order p. 174

Unscramble the sentences. Write them down.

1 Noah · a shower · takes ____________________

2 brushes · his teeth · he ____________________

3 ears · cleans · Noah · his ____________________

4 his · combs · hair · he ____________________

5 takes · perfection · time ____________________

9b grammar: word order p. 174

Unscramble the sentences. Write them down.

1 takes · a shower · Noah · after breakfast ____________________

2 every day · he · his feet · washes ____________________

3 styles · he · after the shower · his hair ____________________

4 the family · Ollie · takes · to the park ____________________

5 his schoolbag · in the evening · packs · Noah ____________________

Challenge: Fill the table with your sentences.

Subjekt	Verb	Objekt	Ergänzung
Noah			

1 DAS VERB BE: AUSSAGEN

the verb be: statements TB p.166

Wenn du über Personen, Tiere oder Dinge sprechen willst, kannst du die Formen *am*, *is* und *are* benutzen.
Sie sind Formen des Verbs *be*. Im gesprochenen Englisch werden sie oft verkürzt.

I am Ava.	→ I'm Ava.
She is eleven.	→ She's eleven.
We are twins.	→ We're twins.

Die Formen von *be* kannst du verneinen, indem du *not* einfügst.
Auch hier gibt es Lang- und Kurzformen.

I am not Ava.	→ I'm not Ava.
She is not eleven.	→ She isn't eleven.
We are not twins.	→ We aren't twins.

2 DAS VERB HAVE GOT: AUSSAGEN

the verb have got: statements TB p.167

Mit *have got* kann man ausdrücken, dass jemand etwas hat oder besitzt. Es gibt auch Kurzformen.

I have got two brothers.	→ I've got two brothers.
He has got a toy.	→ He's got a toy.
We have got a garden.	→ We've got a garden.

Wenn man sagen möchte, dass man etwas nicht hat, stellt man das Wort *not* zwischen *have* und *got* bzw. zwischen *has* und *got*. Die Kurzformen lauten *haven't* und *hasn't*.

I have not got two brothers.	→ I haven't got two brothers.
He has not got a toy.	→ He hasn't got a toy.
We have not got a garden.	→ We haven't got a garden.

3 DAS VERB BE: FRAGEN

the verb be: questions TB p.168

Entscheidungsfragen sind Fragen, die man mit „Ja" oder „Nein" beantworten kann. Wenn du die Entscheidungsfrage mit einer Form von *be* stellen willst, stellst du diese an den Satzanfang. Man antwortet darauf meist mit einer Kurzantwort.

Am I in your team?	Yes, you are.	No, you aren't.
Are you eleven?	Yes, I am.	No, I'm not.
Is he/she/it twelve?	Yes, he/she/it is.	No, he/she/it isn't.
Are they from London?	Yes, they are.	No, they aren't.

Wenn du eine Frage mit Fragewort stellen willst, stellst du das Fragewort an den Anfang. Auch hier werden in gesprochener Sprache häufig Kurzformen verwendet.

What is your name?	→ What's your name?
Where is your friend from?	→ Where's your friend from?
Who is that?	→ Who's that?

4 DAS VERB HAVE GOT: FRAGEN

the verb have got: questions TB p.169

Wenn du eine Entscheidungsfragen mit *have got* oder *has got* stellen möchtest, stellst du *have* oder *has* an den Satzanfang.
Auch hier antwortet man meist mit einer Kurzantwort.

Have I got my phone?	Yes, you have.	No, you haven't.
Have you got a dog?	Yes, I have.	No, I haven't.
Has he/she/it got a brother?	Yes, he/she/it has.	No, he/she/it hasn't.
Have they got a house?	Yes, they have.	No, they haven't.

Wenn du eine Frage mit Fragewort stellen willst, stellst du das Fragewort an den Anfang. Danach folgt dann *have* oder *has*.
Auch hier verwendet man häufig Kurzformen beim Sprechen.

What have you got?	
What have the children got?	
Who has got a dog?	→ Who's got a dog?

5 DIE BEFEHLSFORM

the imperative TB p. 170

So kannst du jemanden um etwas bitten oder auffordern, etwas zu tun (Befehlsform):

Look!
Pack your schoolbag, please.
Be on time, please.
Listen to the teacher, please.

Wenn jemand etwas *nicht* tun soll, kannst du das so sagen (verneinte Befehlsform):

Don't worry!
Don't forget your pencil, please.
Don't be nervous.
Don't play football here, please.

6 DER ARTIKEL

the article TB p. 171

Anders als im Deutschen gibt es im Englischen nur eine Form des bestimmten Artikels: *the*.

the desk	der Schreibtisch	the book	das Buch
the school	die Schule	the chairs	die Stühle

Achtung bei der Aussprache: Wenn das nachfolgende Wort mit einem Vokallaut beginnt, wird *the* nicht /ðə/ ausgesprochen, sondern /ðiː/.

Der unbestimmte Artikel heißt im Englischen *a* und wird /ə/ ausgesprochen. Beginnt das nachfolgende Wort mit einem Vokallaut, verwendest du *an* /ən/.

7 DIE PLURALFORMEN DER NOMEN

the plural forms of nouns TB p. 172

Die meisten englischen Nomen haben im Plural die Endung -s. Achte auf die unterschiedliche Aussprache.

a book one pen	two books /-s/ four pens /-z/	Nach stimmlosen Konsonanten klingt das -s wie ein Zischen, nach stimmhaften Konsonanten wie ein Summen.
a story my hobby	two stories /-ɪz/ my hobbies /-ɪz/	Steht ein Konsonant vor einem -y, so wird das -y im Plural zu -ies.
a box a watch	two boxes /-ɪz/ my watches /-ɪz/	Nomen, die auf -s, -ss, -sh, -ch oder -x enden, erhalten im Plural ein -es.
one foot a child	two feet lots of children	Unregelmäßige Pluralformen lernst du am besten zusammen mit der Singularform.

8 DIE EINFACHE GEGENWART: AUSSAGEN

the simple present: statements TB p. 173

Wenn du ausdrücken willst, dass jemand etwas regelmäßig tut oder dass etwas regelmäßig stattfindet, verwendest du das *simple present*. In der 3. Person Singular *(he, she, it)* hängst du ein -s an.

I meet my friends every Friday.
You like the science club.
We play matches on Saturdays.
They practise on Wednesdays.

The school band meets every Friday.
Lily likes the science club.
Harry plays the guitar.
The football team practises on Wednesdays.

Für die Verneinung fügst du *don't (do not)* bzw. bei der 3. Person Singular *doesn't (does not)* ein.

I don't play football.
You don't play football.
We don't play football
They don't play football.

He/She/It doesn't play football.

9 DIE EINFACHE GEGENWART: FRAGEN

the simple present: questions TB p. 174

Bei Entscheidungsfragen im *simple present* stellst du ein *do* oder *does* an den Satzanfang. Bei der 3. Person Singular hat das Hauptverb dann kein -s. In den Kurzantworten wird *do* oder *does* aufgegriffen.

Do I worry too much?	Yes, you do.	No, you don't.
Do you live in Notting Hill?	Yes, I do.	No, I don't.
Does he/she/it like carrots?	Yes, he/she/it does.	No, he/she/it doesn't.
Do they go to Holland Park School?	Yes, they do.	No, they don't.

Bei Fragen mit Fragewort steht das Fragewort am Satzanfang vor *do* oder *does*.

What do you think about your new school?
When does school start?

10 DIE WORTSTELLUNG IM AUSSAGESATZ

word order in statements TB p. 175

Aussagesätze werden nach einem bestimmten Muster gebildet: Subjekt - Verb - Objekt (S - V - O). Danach können noch weitere Ergänzung stehen.

Subjekt	**Verb**	**Objekt**	**Ergänzung**
Noah	eats	vegetarian sausages.	
Ava	likes	bacon and eggs	for breakfast.
Ava and Noah	meet	their friends	at the weekend.

11 CAN: AUSSAGEN

can: statements TB p. 176

Mit *can* bzw. *can't* kannst du ausdrücken, was jemand tun kann bzw. nicht tun kann.

I can dance, but I can't sing.
You can play football, but you can't play hockey.
Harry can play the guitar, but he can't play the piano.

We can play table tennis, but we can't play tennis.
You can speak English, but you can't speak French.
The children can swim, but they can't ice skate.

12 CAN: FRAGEN

can: questions TB p.177

Wenn du fragen möchtest, was jemand tun oder nicht tun kann, benutzt du *can* bzw. *can't*.
Bei Entscheidungsfragen antwortet man meist mit einer Kurzantwort.

Can I help you?	Yes, you can.	No, you can't.
Can you play the piano?	Yes, I can.	No, I can't.
Can he/she/it swim?	Yes, he/she/it can.	No, he/she/it can't.
Can they speak English?	Yes, they can.	No, they can't.

Bei Fragen mit Fragewort steht das Fragewort am Satzanfang vor *can*.

Where can you play basketball?
When can I go to the park?

13 FRAGEN MIT FRAGEWORT (REVISION)

questions with question words (revision) TB p. 178

Du hast schon gesehen, wie man Fragen mit Fragewort bildet. Hier findest du eine Übersicht.

What do I need? What does Tarek think? Where do the children play?	What have I got? What has Lily got in her schoolbag? What have the children got?
What can I do? When can the children start the game? Where can we play?	Where am I? Who is Tarek's favourite teacher? Where are the children?

14 BESITZVERHÄLTNISSE AUSDRÜCKEN

possessives TB p. 179

Wenn du sagen möchtest, wem oder zu wem etwas gehört, hast du im Englischen verschiedene Möglichkeiten.
Du kannst es z. B. mithilfe des s-Genitivs ausdrücken.

Im Singular hängst du an das Nomen einen Apostroph und ein s an: 's	Bei regelmäßigen Pluralformen fügst du nur den Apostroph an das Plural -s an.	Bei unregelmäßigen Pluralformen, die nicht auf -s enden, hängst du ein 's an.
Tarek's room the girl's room	the girls' room the brothers' parents	the children's room the men's families

Wenn du sagen willst, dass etwas zu einer Sache gehört, kannst du eine Konstruktion mit *of* verwenden:
The name of the school is Holland Park School.

Possessivbegleiter sind Wörter, die man statt eines Nomens mit s-Genitiv verwenden kann:
Ava lives in Notting Hill. Ava's room is small. → Her room ist small.

My house is big.	Our house is big.
Your house is big.	Your house is big.
His/Her/Its house is big.	Their house is big.

15 HÄUFIGKEITSADVERBIEN

adverbs of frequency TB p. 180

Wörter wie *always*, *usually*, *often*, *sometimes* und *never* sind Häufigkeitsadverbien. Mit ihnen kannst du ausdrücken, wie häufig etwas geschieht.

I always tidy the living room.
Lily sometimes cleans the rabbit cage.

My parents usually do the cooking.
You never help!

Bei Sätzen mit *be* stehen die Formen von *be* vor dem Adverb.

I am always hungry.
He is usually at home on Sunday mornings.

We are often in the park.
It is never boring at the swimming pool.

16 DIE VERLAUFSFORM DER GEGENWART: AUSSAGEN

present progressive: statements TB p. 181

Wenn du ausdrücken möchtest, dass jemand etwas jetzt gerade tut oder dass etwas in diesem Moment stattfindet, kannst du das mit der Verlaufsform der Gegenwart tun. Du bildest sie mit einer Form von *be* sowie der Grundform des Verbs *+ing*:

I am opening my presents now.
You are writing text messages.
Noah is buying balloons at the moment.

We are baking biscuits.
Noah and Ava are putting the biscuits on a plate.
They are arriving at the party.

Für die Verneinung fügst du *not* hinter der Form von *be* ein. Hier wird dann häufig die Kurzform verwendet.

I am not making pizza.	→ I'm not making pizza.
Harry is not dancing.	→ Harry isn't dancing.
They are not watching TV.	→ They aren't watching TV.

17 DIE VERLAUFSFORM DER GEGENWART: FRAGEN

present progressive: questions TB p. 182

Mit dem *present progressive* kannst du fragen, was jemand gerade tut. Bei Entscheidungsfragen stellst du eine Form von *be* an den Satzanfang. Man antwortet darauf meist mit einer Kurzantwort.

Am I talking too fast?	Yes, you are.	No, you aren't.
Are you doing your homework?	Yes, I am.	No, I'm not.
Is he/she/it playing?	Yes, he/she/it is.	No, he/she/it isn't.
Are they dancing?	Yes, they are.	No, they aren't.

Bei Fragen mit Fragewort steht das Fragewort am Satzanfang.

What are you doing?
Where are you going?

18 DIE EINFACHE VERGANGENHEIT VON BE

the simple past of be TB p. 183

Wenn du über Vergangenes sprechen möchtest, benutzt du das *simple past*.

I was in Brighton last year.
You were great, Harry!
He was at the beach, too.
Ellen was in Lily's year.
It was brilliant.

We were at home.
You were all scared of the seagull.
The children were at the beach.
They were all really happy.

Für die Verneinung fügst du hinter *was* bzw. *were* ein *not* ein. Auch wird häufig die Kurzform verwendet.

I was not in Brighton.	→ I wasn't in Brighton.
He/She/It was not in Brighton.	→ He/She/It wasn't in Brighton.
They were not in Brighton.	→ They weren't in Brighton.

Die Fragen in der Vergangenheit werden analog zur Gegenwart gebildet.

Was Noah in Brighton last year?
Were the children in Brighton last year?
Where were the children?

LANGUAGE HELP — Objektpronomen

Die Objektpronomen *me, you, him, her, it, us, you, them* kannst du als Objekt eines Satzes verwenden.

Beispiel: *Noah combs his hair. He combs it every day.*

They take him to the park

10 grammar: word order p. 175

Rewrite the sentences. Underline the object in green.

1 Noah takes a shower after breakfast. *Noah takes it after breakfast.*

2 He washes his feet every day. ______

3 He styles his hair after the shower. ______

4 The family takes Ollie to the park. ______

5 Noah packs his schoolbag in the evening. ______

Weekend activities

11 wordbank: free time p. 157

Collect ideas for weekend activities.

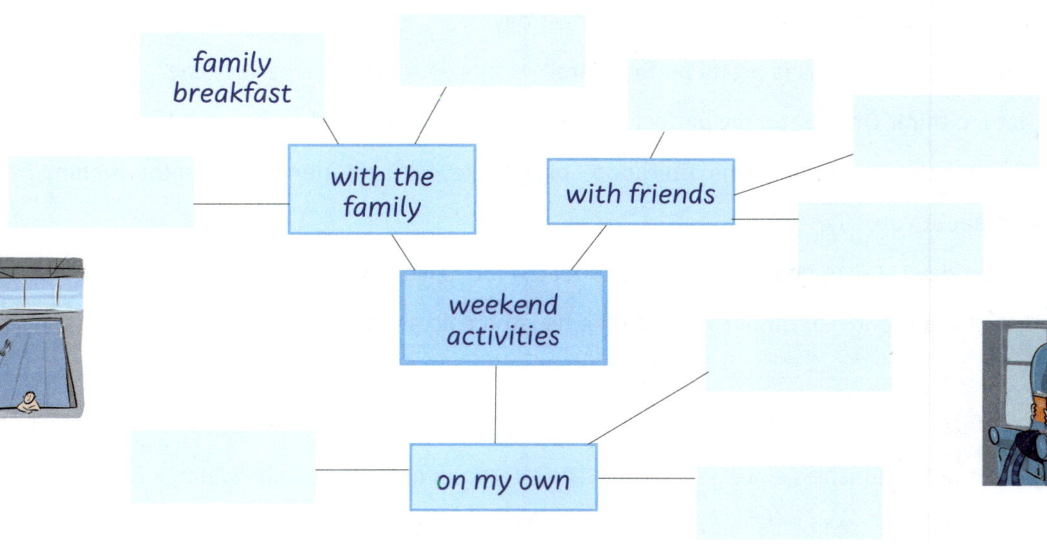

More weekend activities

12 CHOOSE YOUR TASK audio 1/57

A **Write a weekend planner for yourself.**

B **Design a weekend planner for a dog.**

C **Listen to the podcast "Weekend fun" and take notes in German: Von welcher Zeit erzählt der Mann? Welche Aktivitäten erwähnt er?**

Practise reading

Tipp 5
Es kann dir helfen, während des Lesens einen Text durch Unterstreichungen oder Markierungen zu strukturieren.

What a perfect day!

13a

Look at the text. Write down the names of the children. Choose a colour for each child.

Ava ______ ______ ______ ______ ______

13b

Now read the text. What is it about? Tick ☑.

☐ the best hobbies ☐ a perfect day ☐ weekend plans

13c audio 1/59

What do the children say about their perfect day? Use your colours from 13a.

Ava: Sunshine, friends and watermelon – what a perfect day!

Harry: Yeah, you're right, Ava. This is pretty perfect. Tarek, what's your idea of a perfect day?

Tarek: Hmm, let me think. Oh, yes, on my perfect day I make lunch for my dad and my uncle. I make their favourite meal – and they clean up! In the afternoon I play hockey with my friends. And in the evening I stay up really late. What about you, Lily?

Lily: On my perfect day I stay in bed all morning and read a lot. I also play with my rabbits. In the afternoon I go to a flea market with a friend. For dinner we go to the fish and chip shop and then we play board games in the evening.

Noah: On my perfect day I sleep in. For breakfast I have pancakes. Then I meet my friends in the park. First we play football and then, at lunchtime, we eat pizza. In the afternoon my friends and I watch a film together.

Harry: And don't forget ice cream! It's not a perfect day without ice cream!

Lily: That's true, Harry! And on your perfect day you play the guitar, listen to loud music and play computer games, right?

Harry: Yeah, on my perfect day I do what I want.

PRACTISE READING

Hat **Tipp 5** dir geholfen, den Text zu verstehen? ◯ ja ◯ teilweise ◯ nein

My perfect day at the weekend TARGET TASK SUPPORT

14

1 What is important for a perfect day at the weekend? Collect ideas in the table.

activities	food	people	places	weather

2 Complete the sentences. Then choose the sentences you want to use in your text.

My perfect day at the weekend

On my perfect day I get up at ______ *. I want to do* ______ .

The weather is ______ *. In the morning* ______ .

For breakfast I have ______ *. Then I go to* ______

with my ______ *. After that I play* ______ .

For lunch I have ______ *. I make* ______

for ______ *. In the afternoon I go to* ______ .

For dinner ______ *. In the evening I stay up really late.*

I play ______ *. I go to bed at* ______ .

That is my perfect day at the weekend.

Tipp: Überprüfe deinen Text

1 Hast du alles aufgeschrieben, was dir wichtig ist? Möchtest du noch etwas hinzufügen?
2 Hast du dir von deinen Klassenkameraden und -kameradinnen Feedback geben lassen? Überlege, was du davon umsetzen kannst.
3 Sieh dir deinen Text noch einmal genau an. Gibt es Wörter, die du noch einmal überprüfen möchtest? Achte dabei auf die Bedeutung und die Schreibweise.
4 Bist du mit der Grammatik unsicher? Schau im Grammatikteil im Textbook noch einmal nach.
5 Falls nötig, schreibe eine zweite, verbesserte Version deines Textes.
6 Für die Präsentation ist es gut, wenn alles schön aussieht. Achte auch darauf.

Free time activities

1

Talk to your classmates. Find someone who does the activities.

draw pictures · play hockey · read books · play in a band · play board games · swim · collect comics · watch films at the cinema · play video games · play with your pet · go skateboarding · dance · ...

You can ask:
Do you draw pictures?
Do you play hockey?

You can answer:
Yes, sometimes.
No, but I swim.

Favourite hobbies

2a audio 2/1

Listen to the children in TB2a again. Which hobbies are they talking about? Tick ✓ .

☐ playing computer games →	☐ cooking →	☐ skateboarding →	☐ riding a bike
☐ music →	☐ taking pictures →	☐ playing the guitar →	☐ singing
☐ playing an instrument →	☐ dancing →	☐ shopping →	☐ team sports

2b CHOOSE YOUR LEVEL

I Complete the fact file about Ava. II Complete two of the fact files. III Complete the fact files.

Ava	Tarek
Ava can't ______	Tarek's favourite hobby is ______
She likes ______	He goes ______
She can do some ______	He can ______
Her best ______ is the kickflip.	His ______ is lasagna.
Harry	**Lily**
Harry's hobby is ______	Lily likes ______, too.
He can ______	She ______
He can't ______	She ______
His favourite ______ is rock music.	Her ______ style is streetdance.
He ______	She doesn't ______

A hobby survey

3a grammar: can questions p. 177

Ask three classmates what they can do. Take notes.

You can ask:
Can you play table tennis?
Can you …?

You can answer:
Yes, I can.
No, I can't.

name											?

3b grammar: can statements p. 176

Write about the answers or present them in class.

Jarek can ride a horse. He can sing, but he can't ice-skate.

Sound check

4a audio 2/3

Learn to say the letters 'ea'. Listen and repeat the words.

team · great · meal · please · weather · leave · breakfast · read · wear · speak · ice cream

4b

Listen again. Underline the words with the long /i:/ sound.

4c audio 2/4

Listen and check your words.

More fun activities

5 CHOOSE YOUR LEVEL grammar: can statements p. 176

I **Look at the pictures in TB4 again. Write what you can or can't do.**

1 I ______ swim.
2 ______
3 ______
4 ______
5 ______
6 ______

II **Complete the sentences with can or can't.**

1 You ______ ride a horse in a bathroom.
2 You ______ do gymnastics in the gym.
3 You ______ play the piano on the bus.
4 Without a ball you ______ play table tennis.
5 In winter you ______ go ice-skating.
6 You ______ climb a tree in the water.

III **Write about what the people can ✓ and can't X do.**

1 Bob: dance ✓ play tennis X *Bob can dance, but he can't play tennis.*
2 Leila: ride a bike ✓ play the guitar X ______
3 Eva: climb a tree X play football ✓ ______
4 Fred: play handball X run fast ✓ ______
5 Judy: draw pictures ✓ sing X ______
6 Paul: ice-skate X jump very high ✓ ______

Challenge: Write funny sentences with can't in your exercise book. *You can't eat a skateboard.*

My favourite sport

6 CHOOSE YOUR LEVEL video 11

Watch the video clip again. I Answer questions 1-3. II Answer questions 1-4. III Answer questions 1-5.

	Gracie	Amy	Sophia
1 How old are the girls?			
2 What's their sport?			
3 How often do they do it?			
4 What do they need for their sport?			
5 Why do they like it?			

Team table tennis

7 skill: mediation p. 145

Deine Freundin sieht die Beschreibung von *Team table tennis*. Hilf ihr, die Regeln zu verstehen.

1 Wie viele Spieler dürfen mitspielen?

2 Wo spielt man das Spiel?

3 Was passiert, wenn man den Ball nicht trifft?

4 Wie gewinnt man das Spiel?

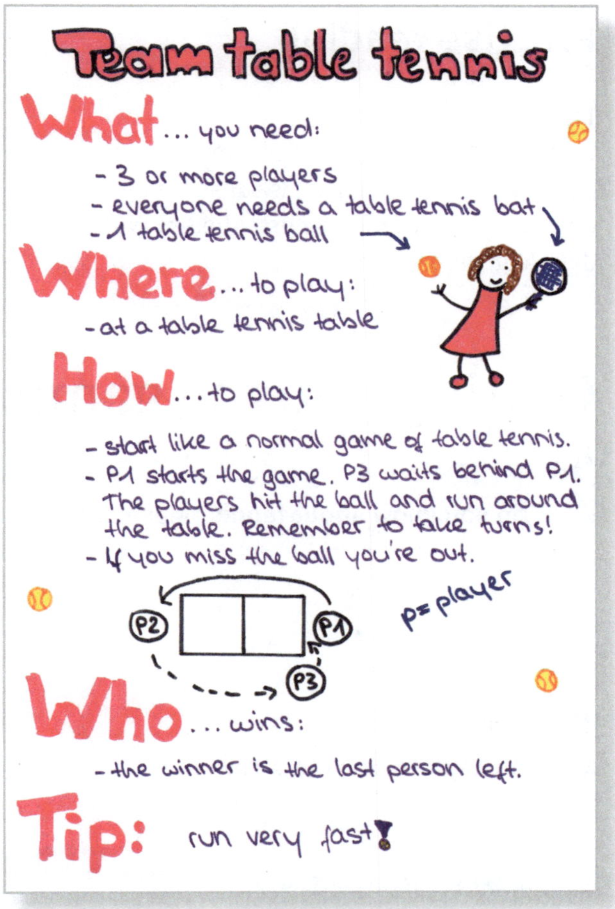

Anton's hobby

8 CHOOSE YOUR LEVEL

Anton's hobby is collecting things. Look at the picture. Make notes. Talk about it and record yourself. Edit the recording. I Talk for 20 seconds. II Talk for 40 seconds. III Talk for 60 seconds.

You can say:
I can see …
Anton's got …
There are many …
He collects …
I think he really likes …
I like …, too.
I (also) collect …
I don't collect …

Practise reading

Tipp 6
Versuche die Wörter, die du beim Lesen nicht gleich verstehst, aus dem Textzusammenhang oder aus der Situation zu erschließen. Nutze dabei dein Allgemeinwissen.

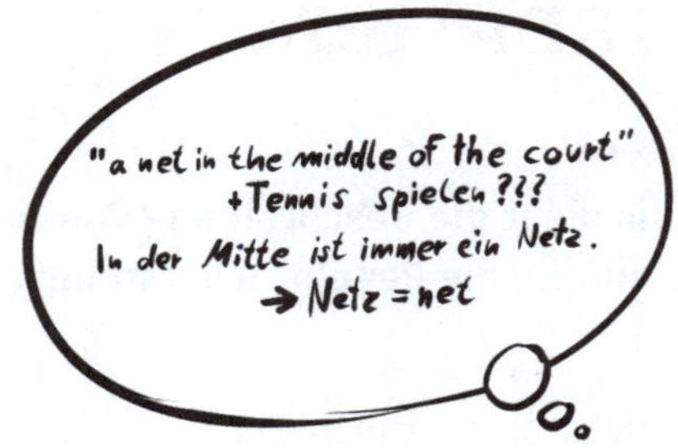

Getting into the game

9a

What do you know about tennis? Make notes.

9b audio 2/8

Read the text. Follow the arrows.

„two or four" gehört zu „players" → Ich weiß, dass es im Tennis zwei oder vier Spieler gibt. → Dann muss „players" eigentlich „Spieler" heißen.

Tennis is a ball game for two or four players. Every player needs a tennis racket. You play tennis on a tennis court. There is a net in the middle of the court. One player hits the ball over the net with his or her racket. The other player tries to hit it back over the net. It is important to keep the ball inside the lines. You get a point if the other player can't hit the ball back or hits the ball out.

In der Mitte des Feldes ist ein Netz, also wird „net" wohl „Netz" heißen. → Was spielt sich am Netz ab? → Der Ball wird über das Netz geschlagen: „hit the ball over the net".

9c

Read the text about video games. Circle the words you don't know. Then do the same as in 9b.

A lot of people play video games in their free time. You can play alone or with other players and you can play offline or online. You need a computer, a console, a tablet or a smartphone. There are lots of different kinds of video games, for example sports games or simulations.

9d

Look up the words. Were you right?

PRACTISE READING

Hat **Tipp 6** dir geholfen, den Text zu verstehen? ◯ ja ◯ teilweise ◯ nein

Playing rugby

10a audio 2/9

Listen and read along.

Rugby is a team sport. There are different versions of rugby. In standard rugby, there are two teams of 15 players. You play rugby on a rugby field. There are two field goals that look like the letter "H". You also need a rugby ball. A rugby ball is not round like a football – it looks like an egg. Each team tries to get the ball behind the other team's field goal. The players can kick, throw and catch the ball. They can tackle other players to take the ball from them. The team scores points when a player puts the ball on or behind the other team's goal line, or kicks the ball over the field goal.

10b

Read the questions. Underline the answers in the text.

1 What kind of sport is it?
2 How many players are there?
3 Where do you play it?
4 What do you need?
5 What can you do with the ball?
6 When do you score a point?

Another hobby

11a audio 2/10, numbers p. 232

Maths can be another hobby. Do you know the numbers? Listen and circle the numbers you hear.

15	60	→	57	75	→	80	18	→	92	29	→	12	21
42	24	→	13	30	→	28	82	→	17	70	→	36	63

11b audio 2/11

Listen to the numbers and write them down like this.

49 forty-nine ______ → ______ → ______

______ → ______ → ______

Who can play?

12 grammar: can questions p. 177

Write questions for the answers. Use the question words.

1 Tarek can play hockey. Who ______

2 Ava can do a kickflip. What ______

3 You can't swim in the gym. Where ______

5 We can go home after school. When ______

6 Lars can't play table tennis. What ______

Sound check

13 audio 2/12

Learn to say the letter 'i'. Listen to the words and repeat them. What do you notice?

picture · little · time · milk · girl · drink · idea · sunshine · thirteen · climb · piano · first · middle · behind

Your favourite activity

14 CHOOSE YOUR LEVEL wordbank: free time p. 157

I Write about your favourite activity. Tick ✓ or write your answer.

My favourite activity is ______ .

I like it because

☐ I'm good at it. ☐ my friends like it, too.

I do it. ☐ I watch it live or on TV. ☐

You do it ☐ inside. ☐ outside.

You need ☐ a ball. ☐ special clothes.

II Write about your favourite activity.

What is your favourite activity? ______

Where do you do it? ______

When do you do it? ______

What clothes do you need? ______

______

What else do you need? ______

III Write about your favourite activity in your exercise book.

Present a sport or hobby TARGET TASK SUPPORT

15 wordbank: free time p. 157, skill: presentations p. 146

1 Collect information about your sport or hobby. Take notes.

What is it? ______________________

How often do you do it? ______________________

Do you do or play it alone or with others? ______________________

What do you do? OR Explain the rules. ______________________

Where do you do or play it? ______________________

____

What do you need? ______________________

What else is important? ______________________

How long have you been doing it? ______________________

What do you want to bring to class? ______________________

2 Complete the sentences. Choose the sentences you want to use.

Beginning: Hello everybody. My presentation is about ______________________.

I want to talk about ______________________. My sport is ______________________.

My favourite hobby is ______________________.

Main part: You can play it with ______________________. I often go to ______________________.

The best place for it is ______________________. I've been doing it for ______ years.

You need ______________________ and ______________________.

You have to ______________________. You can ______________________.

You can't ______________________. You play it with ______________________

You win when ______________________. It ends when ______________________.

I love it because ______________________.

End: Thank you for listening. Have you got any questions?

Tipp: Bei einer Präsentation frei sprechen

Frei zu sprechen ist gar nicht so einfach. Aber es macht Spaß, jemandem zuzuhören, der frei sprechen kann. Deshalb lohnt es sich, frei sprechen zu üben.

1. Mach dir Notizen für deine Präsentation.
2. Nimm dir genügend Zeit.
3. Überlege dir ein paar einfache Sätze, die auch nicht zu lang sind.
4. Übe deine Präsentation zunächst alleine.
5. Dann übe mit einem Partner oder einer Partnerin. Denkt daran, langsam, laut und deutlich zu sprechen. Schaut einander beim Sprechen an.

Die Check out-Seiten helfen dir einzuschätzen, was du schon gut kannst und was du noch üben solltest.
Löse die Aufgaben auf dieser Doppelseite und male die Kreise wie auf Seite 28 rot, gelb oder grün aus.

1 Kannst du dich über Frühstücksgewohnheiten unterhalten?
2 Kannst du beschreiben, was jemand am Wochenende macht?
3 Kannst du eine kurze Sprachnachricht zu einer Verabredung verstehen?
4 Kannst du ausdrücken, was jemand tun kann oder nicht tun kann?
5 Kannst du Hobbys und Sportarten benennen und beschreiben?
6 Kannst du einen kurzen Text zu einem Hobby oder einer Sportart verstehen?

1

Talk to a partner. Ask and answer questions. Take turns. You can make a recording.

- What do you have for breakfast before school?
- What do you have for breakfast at the weekend?
- What do you drink with your breakfast?
- What is a perfect breakfast for you?
  - When and where is it?
  - Who is there?
  - What do you eat and drink?

Ich kann mich über Frühstücksgewohnheiten unterhalten. ○

2

Look at the planner on Harry's mobile phone. Write about his plans for the weekend.

SAT	SUN
9:30am: breakfast with Tarek and his dad	1pm: dinner at an Indian restaurant (family)
5pm: watch a film at the Electric Cinema with Lily	afternoon: play board games with Ava and Lily

Ich kann beschreiben, was jemand am Wochenende macht. ○

3 audio 2/13

Lily wants to meet Ava. Listen to her voice message and tick ✓ the right answer.

1 Where does Lily want to meet Ava?
- ☐ in the park
- ☐ at her place
- ☐ at Ava's place

2 What does Lily want to do with Ava?
- ☐ listen to music and play video games
- ☐ go skateboarding
- ☐ listen to music and play with the rabbits

3 When does she want to meet Ava?
- ☐ at 12pm
- ☐ at 2pm
- ☐ at 4pm

Ich kann eine kurze Sprachnachricht zu einer Verabredung verstehen. ○

4

What can Alfie do? What can't he do? Write about him.

+ swim fast · climb high walls · draw pictures	- make lunch · ride a horse · play rugby
Alfie ______	Alfie ______
He ______	He ______
______	______

Ich kann ausdrücken, was jemand tun kann oder nicht tun kann. ◯

5

Read the sentences and fill in the missing words.

1 You can do gymnastics and play handball in a _ _ _ .

2 Football players kick the ball into a _ _ _ _ .

3 My brother and I like to go ice-skating at the _ _ _ _ _ _ _ .

4 You can play tennis with a _ _ _ _ _ _ .

5 Are you good at running?
Then you can do _ _ _ _ _ _ _ _ _ .

6 Do you like water and swimming?
Then you can go to the _ _ _ _ _ _ _ _ _ _ _ _ .

Ich kann Hobbys und Sportarten benennen und beschreiben. ◯

6

Read about Mia's hobbies. Then tick ✓ true or false.

I have two hobbies: playing the guitar and doing karate.

I practise the guitar every day after school. On Tuesdays, I have lessons at the music school. My teacher, Ms Greene, is really nice. I am in the school band, too. We are twelve students and it is great fun to play music together.

On Mondays, I go to the karate club. Our teacher, Mr Kurosawa, is from Japan. He shows us many different moves. I learn a lot from him. I want to be really good at karate, too.

	true	false
1 Mia plays two instruments.	☐	☐
2 She has guitar lessons on Mondays.	☐	☐
3 She plays in the school band.	☐	☐
4 Her guitar teacher is from Japan.	☐	☐
5 There are ten students in the school band.	☐	☐
6 At the karate club, Mia learns a lot from Mr Kurosawa.	☐	☐

Ich kann einen kurzen Text zu einem Hobby oder einer Sportart verstehen. ◯

Wenn du noch mehr üben möchtest, gehe zu Practise more - Unit 3. DIGITAL+

Saturday afternoon

1

Look at the picture and answer the questions.

1 Who is in the picture? ____________________

____

2 What's the weather like? ____________________

3 What else can you see? ____________________

____

4 What do you think? What is the situation? Tick ✓

☐ The children are quiet.
☐ They are happy.
☐ The day is boring.
☐ They are waiting for someone.
☐ They want something.
☐ ____________________

At Uncle Sami's house

2 CHOOSE YOUR LEVEL

Tarek, his dad and Uncle Sami discuss what they want to do.
Match the phrases. There is more than one way to do it.

Match four phrases.
Match six phrases.
Match the phrases.

1 There's a football game on at 3pm. Let's watch it!
2 Who wants to watch a film?
3 Do you know the new quiz show *Domino*? It starts today.
4 Hey, who wants to watch videos?
5 I would like to watch the news in half an hour.
6 What about the tennis game at 4pm?
7 Let's watch some cat videos.
8 I could show you some videos with cool dance moves.

A I don't, but let's check it out. It sounds cool!
B I don't know – I'm not a football fan.
C Great idea! I love tennis.
D Yeah, why not. I like cats.
E Oh no, that's boring.
F Sounds good.
G Yeah, OK then.
H Hm, I'm not sure. Maybe we could watch basketball.

1	B
2	
3	
4	
5	
6	
7	
8	

Getting ready for the game

3 audio 2/15, skill: listening p. 141

Listen to Lily and her mum. Tick ✓ the correct answer.

1 Why does Lily want to find her mum?
- ☐ She wants to help her with dinner.
- ☐ She wants some milk.
- ☐ She wants to ask her about buying snacks.

2 Where is Lily's mum?
- ☐ in the bathroom
- ☐ in the kitchen
- ☐ in her office

3 Where does Lily want to buy snacks?
- ☐ at the corner shop
- ☐ at the café
- ☐ at the market

4 How much money does Lily's mum give Lily?
- ☐ 5 pounds
- ☐ 10 pounds
- ☐ 20 pounds

5 What time is dinner?
- ☐ at 7 o'clock
- ☐ at 6 o'clock
- ☐ at 8 o'clock

6 What does Lily have to do before dinner?
- ☐ do her homework
- ☐ escape
- ☐ come home from shopping

Challenge: **Use the correct answers to write about the dialogue.**
Lily wants to find her mum. She wants to ask her about …

The weather

4a

Collect weather words.

4b

Write about what you can do …

in hot weather: *I can sit in the sun. I can* ____________________

in rainy weather: ____________________

in windy weather: ____________________

in cold weather: ____________________

Questions

5 CHOOSE YOUR LEVEL grammar: questions with question words p. 178

What do you know about the children and Notting Hill?

I Complete the questions.

what · where · how · when · who

1 ______ old is Harry?

2 ______ pets have Lily and Harry got?

3 ______ can cook?

4 ______ do the children go to school?

5 ______ does school start?

II Complete the questions in I and answer them.

1 ______

2 ______

3 ______

4 ______

5 ______

III Write five questions and answer them. Use can, do, be and have got.

1 *Where* ______

2 *Who* ______

3 *How* ______

4 *What* ______

5 *When* ______

Practise reading

Tipp 7

Denke nach, bevor du liest! Es hilft dir oft, wenn du überlegst, was du schon über ein Thema weißt, bevor du einen Text darüber liest.

In the corner shop

6a

Circle the words and phrases you expect in a text about shopping.

milk · we need · pay · where are · socks · please · ice cream · biscuits · how much

flavour · comic · bottles · let's get · buy · apples · crisps · on the shelf · thank you

6b audio 2/16

Read the text. Find the words you expected. Circle them.

Harry: Ava, can you get three bottles of lemonade, please? They're at the back behind the water bottles.

Ava: Yes, of course.

Harry: Let's get some crisps, Tarek. We always get salt and vinegar. What flavour would you like?

Tarek: Cheese and onion, please.

Harry: OK. They're here, between the chocolate and the biscuits.

Lily: Let's get some ice cream, too!

Tarek: Ice cream is over there in the freezer next to the fridge. Is chocolate OK?

Ava: Oh, yes, please. I love chocolate ice cream!

Lily: Good. And there's the milk, too. We also need lemons – but I can only see bananas. – Excuse me, Mr Hu, where are the lemons, please?

Mr Hu: Oh, they're here on the shelf, above the melons. In front of the oranges.

Lily: Thanks a lot!

Harry: Hey guys, have you got everything?

Ava: Yes, we have.

Lily: OK, let's pay then.

6c

Underline the food and drink words in the text.

PRACTISE READING

Hat **Tipp 7** dir geholfen, den Text zu verstehen? ◯ ja ◯ teilweise ◯ nein

Is that everything?

7a audio 2/17, skill: talking with people p. 142

Listen to the phrases and read along. What does a shopkeeper[1] say? What does a customer[2] say? Write S for shopkeeper or C for customer or B for both[3] next to each phrase.

Is that everything?	S	Here you are.	
How much are the crisps?		Could I have a bottle of apple juice, please?	
Hello!		Thank you very much for your help.	
They are over there, next to the apples.		You're welcome!	
The crisps are one pound forty.		Have a nice evening.	
How much is it?		Thanks a lot!	
Can I help you?		Excuse me. Where are the oranges, please?	
That's 7 pounds 80 pence, please.		Thank you. Bye, children!	

1 shopkeeper – Ladeninhaber/in, **2 customer** – Kunde/Kundin, **3 both** – beide

7b CHOOSE YOUR LEVEL

skill: talking with people p. 142

Work with a partner. Choose one or more of the short dialogues. Act them out.
I Act out one of the dialogues. II Act out two of the dialogues. III Act out the dialogues.

1
- Hello!
- Good morning!
- Can I help you?
- How much are the crisps?
- The crisps are one pound forty.

2
- Could I have a bottle of water, please?
- Here you are.
- Thanks a lot!
- Is that everything?
- Yes, that's all today.

3
- Excuse me. Where are the oranges, please?
- They are over there, next to the apples.
- Thank you very much for your help.
- You're welcome!

4
- How much is it?
- That's 7 pounds 80 pence, please.
- Thank you. Bye, children!
- Bye. Have a nice day.

At night at the corner shop

8a

audio 2/18, wordbank: places p. 152

Where are the mice[1]? Listen and number the pairs of mice[2] in the correct order.

1 mouse (pl mice) – Maus, 2 pairs of mice – Mäusepaare

8b

Listen again and write down where the mice are.

1 The mice are *between the carrots and the apples.*

2 The mice are ______

3 The mice are ______

4 The mice are ______

5 The mice are ______

6 The mice are ______

Shopping for food

9 CHOOSE YOUR TASK audio 2/19, wordbank: food p. 156

Draw or write the food and drink words into the trolley.

A **What are your favourite snacks for a rainy afternoon?**

B **Listen to the people at the corner shop. What do they buy?**

C **Read the recipe. Write down in German what you have to buy.**

Grannie's Favourite Apple Crumble Recipe

Heat the oven to 190°. Slice three apples.
Mix them with two tablespoons of brown sugar.
Put them in a baking dish.
Put 175g of flour, 110g butter and 110g brown sugar in a bowl with a pinch of salt.
Mix well with your fingers.
Crumble the mix over the apples.
Put it in the oven for 30-35 minutes.
Enjoy it with vanilla ice cream!

A tidy bedroom

10a

Label the picture with the words in the blue boxes.

shelves · floor · board game · bed · rabbits · skateboard · lamp · sock · poster · cage · guitar

10b grammar: possessives p. 179

Whose is it? Fill in the gaps.

1 ______________ poster shows a football team.

2 ______________ bed is grey.

3 ______________ board game is on the floor.

4 ______________ guitar is in front of his bed.

5 ______________ rabbits are in their cage.

6 ______________ skateboard is on the shelves.

Lily's ·
Harry's ·
Lily and Harry's

Your room

11a
wordbank: at home p. 158

Draw your room and label it.

11b
video 14

Watch the video clip in TB9a again. Number the sentences in the right order.

- ☐ This is my bookcase where I keep ...
- ☐ Behind me is my favourite ...
- ☐ And this is where I do my homework.
- ☐ This is my bedroom.
- ☐ I like my bedroom because ...
- ☐ That was my room. I hope you liked it.
- ☐ And this is my bed.
- ☐ This is my wardrobe.
- ☐ Next to my ... is my schoolbag.

11c
skill: presentations p. 146

Present your room. Use the phrases in 11b. You can use your drawing or make a video.

LANGUAGE HELP Possessivbegleiter TB S. 179 14b)

Possessivbegleiter stehen vor einem Nomen. Sie drücken aus, wem oder zu wem etwas gehört.
Beispiele: *my* mother, *your* hair, *our* bedroom

Next to the door

12 CHOOSE YOUR LEVEL
grammar: possessive determiners p. 179, wordbank: places p. 152

I Write four or more sentences. II Write six or more sentences. III Write eight or more sentences.

Our Their My Your His Her Its	shelves wardrobe cage ...	is are	next to under between in in front of behind on	the window. the shelves and the wardrobe. the cage. the carpet. ...

Sound check

13
audio 2/22

Learn to say the sound /əʊ/.
Listen to the words and repeat them.

home · phone · own · alone · oh · poster · moment · mango · go · hotel · no · comb

Fun activities at home TARGET TASK SUPPORT

14 wordbank: free time p. 157, skill: searching the Internet p. 148, writing p. 143

1 What is a podcast?

A podcast is a bit like a personal radio show. What is different? You find podcasts on the Internet. People can listen to them when they have the time.

2 Collect some activities.

go on a treasure hunt, read a story to your friends, decorate biscuits, ____________

____

____

3 Complete the sentences. Then choose the sentences you want to use in your presentation.

Introduction:

Hi everyone! Hi and welcome to ____________

It's podcast time again! My name is ____________ and I'm your host today.

Today I want to talk about ____________.

This podcast is about ____________.

Main part:

Let's start with ____________. You can play it alone or ____________.

You could ____________. Let me tell you how ____________ works.

You need ____________.

You could also ____________. Why don't you ____________?

What other games can you play? Well, what about ____________?

End:

So you see, there are a lot of fun ____________ for a rainy day.
I hope you like some of the ideas. That's it for today.
That's all from me for today. Thank you for listening. Bye guys!

Tipp: Eine gute Audio-Aufnahme machen

Am besten machst du die Aufnahme mit deinem Handy.

1 Achte darauf, dass du keine unerwünschten Nebengeräusche aufnimmst.

2 Den Zuhörern soll es Freude machen, deinen Podcast anzuhören. Deshalb achte zunächst auf eine gute Klangqualität. Nimm den Anfang deines Textes zur Probe auf. Probiere aus, wie sich die Qualität verändert, wenn du das Mikrofon etwas näher an den Mund hältst oder weiter entfernt.

3 Prüfe dann, ob du flüssig, verständlich und langsam genug gesprochen hast. Wenn du dir bei der Aussprache eines Wortes nicht sicher bist, kannst du es dir in einem Online-Wörterbuch anhören und nachsprechen.

4 Nimm dann deinen Text Absatz für Absatz auf. Höre deine Aufnahme zwischendurch an und nimm den Absatz erneut auf, wenn du noch nicht zufrieden bist.

Jobs at home

1 wordbank: at home p. 158

Match the words in the boxes.

~~bake~~ · clean · do · do · tidy · cook · wash make

the bathroom · ~~a cake~~ · the shopping · the living room · dinner · the plates · the bed · the cooking

bake a cake ____ ____ ____

____ ____ ____ ____

Who says what?

2

Read TB1 again. Write A for Ava or D for Dad next to the sentences.

1 Is it OK if I stay here for another half hour? ☐

2 Yes, that's fine. ☐

3 He's not home. ☐

4 I'm at Harry and Lily's place. ☐

5 But make sure you're home at seven, please. ☐

6 Could you take Ollie for a walk this evening? ☐

7 Can't Noah do it? ☐

8 And it's Mum's day to work late. ☐

Mum's message

3

Complete the text messages with phrases from the box.

empty the dishwasher · do the cooking · does the shopping · empty the dishwasher · do the shopping for Granny · buy some tomatoes · go to the supermarket

Mum: Hey Noah, where are you? Could you ____ for dinner? Love, Mum.

Noah: I'm at Tarek's place. Can't Ava do it?

Mum: She's not home. You know that Ava always ____ for the neighbours on Tuesdays.

Noah: What about Dad then?

Mum: No, it's his day to work late and my day to ____!

Noah: I always ____. And it's my turn to ____ today. What about Joshua?

Mum: Joshua is only six! He can't ____ alone. I can ____ for you today, OK? But please hurry with the tomatoes. Thank you!

Noah: OK!

Challenge: **Write text messages like this in your exercise book. Read them out with a partner.**

A chores survey

4a CHOOSE YOUR LEVEL wordbank: at home p. 158, time p. 155

I Which chores do you do? How often? Do you like them? Tick ✓ ☺ or ☹.

chores I do / how often	☺	☹
vacuum my bedroom / sometimes		✓

II Ask a classmate about his or her chores. Do they like them? Tick ✓ ☺ or ☹.

name	how often?	chores	☺	☹
	always	*makes*		
	sometimes			
	never			
	usually			
	often			

III Talk to two or more classmates about their chores. Take notes. Then write about your and your classmates' chores in your exercise book.

You can write:

My chores are to make my bed and … I often … I like it. Marie usually … She …

4b audio 2/24

Listen to the chores survey. Who does what? How often? Fill in the lists.

	vacuum? / how often?	clean kitchen? / how often?	tidy? / how often?
Rita's family			
Ben's family			
Lotta's family			

LANGUAGE HELP — die einfache Gegenwart: 3. Person Singular TB. S. 173

Besonderheiten der 3. Person Singular: Endet das Verb auf -ss, -sh, -ch oder -x, hängst du ein -*es* an.
Beispiel: *washes*, *touches*

Auch bei *do* und *go* hängst du ein -*es* an. *does*, *goes*

Bei Verben, die auf y enden, gilt diese Regel: Kommt ein Konsonant vor dem y, wird das y zu -*ies*. Beispiel: *hurries*

Sound check

5 audio 2/25, grammar: simple present statements p. 173

Write down the 3rd person singular forms of the verbs. Then listen and repeat.

do – ____________ → *go –* ____________

try – ____________ → *empty –* ____________

guess – ____________ → *finish –* ____________

Chores for the ghost family

6a

Unscramble the sentences about the chores for the ghost family.

1 sometimes · in his bedroom · Billy · cleans the cage ____________

2 vacuums · the living room · always · Milly ____________

3 Vanilly · in the kitchen · sets the table · usually ____________

4 tidies · often · the living room · Zilly ____________

5 cleans · never · Pilly · the bathroom ____________

6b grammar: adverbs of frequency p. 180

Who does what in your family? Write down questions and answer them.

Who usually empties the dishwasher? – That's me!

____

____

____

____

____

____

____

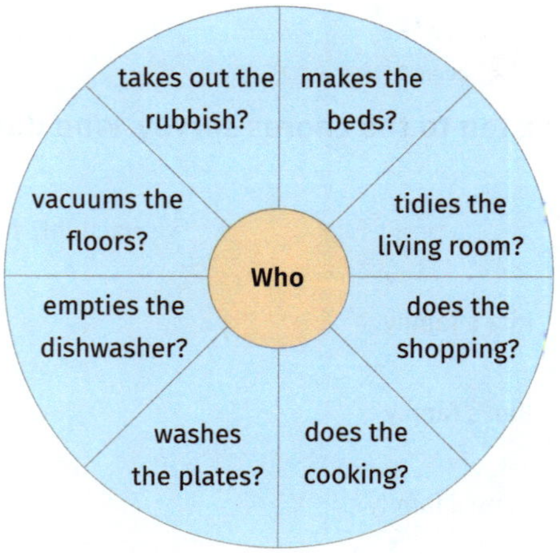

Where is Ollie?

7 wordbank: places p. 152

Ollie is at home alone. Where is he? Write sentences.

on · in · behind · in front of · under · next to

1 *Ollie is* ______

2 *He is* ______

3 ______

4 ______

5 ______

6 ______

Don McClean in action

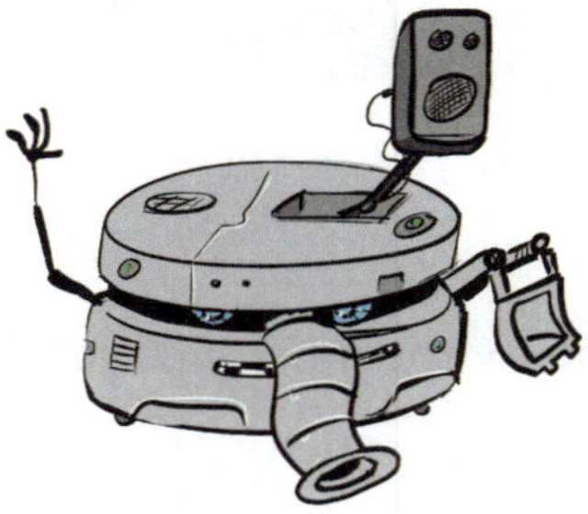

8a audio 2/27

Listen to what Don McClean does in Mr Dull's house. Which rooms does the robot go into?

______

______

8b CHOOSE YOUR LEVEL skill: writing p. 143

Listen again and make notes. Write about Mr Dull's robot in your exercise book.

- I Write four sentences.
- II Write six sentences.
- III Write eight sentences or more.

Practise reading

Tipp 8
Überfliege einen langen Text zuerst. Schaue dir die Zwischenüberschriften und Bilder an. Dann suche im Text gezielt nach Wörtern, die zu den Bildern passen *(scan the text)*. Lies dabei nicht jedes Wort.

Ollie's week

9a

Look at the five pictures and read the words in the box. Find the things in the pictures.

kitchen · dog school · homework · mum · cooking · skateboard · garden · living room · dad · park · sofa kitchen · friends · brother · dogs

9b audio 2/29

Look at the picture and scan the text. What belongs together?

1

Monday

Hello, I'm Ollie! I'm a dog and I live with Ava and her family. I want to tell you about my week and all my chores. On Monday afternoon my chores begin when the children come back from school. I take Ava for a walk to the park. We usually practise skateboarding. I teach her tricks on the skateboard.

9c audio 2/30

Do the same for the other pictures and texts.

2

Tuesday

Tuesday is a good day for me. I go to dog school and meet my friends there. We always do a lot of fun activities together and I usually get lots of treats. That's a good chore because it's a lot of fun. But I have to look after Ava because sometimes she is too nice to the other dogs!

Wednesday

Wednesday is spaghetti day! It's great! When Ava comes home, we always eat spaghetti. On Wednesdays, Ava often has a lot of homework and I'm in the garden. I have to dig holes and look for squirrels. That's very important!

Thursday

On Thursdays, I usually look after Ava and her little brother, Joshua. In the evening, Ava sometimes helps her mum with the cooking but Joshua never helps. Ava says that's OK because he's only six but that's no excuse. I'm only four and I've got a lot of chores!

Friday

Ava is often away on Friday afternoons. But I've got my chores! I have to look after Joshua and the rest of the family. Ava's dad usually does the cooking and cleans the kitchen. After dinner, Ava's mum often makes plans for the weekend and I help her and tell her my ideas for family time.

PRACTISE READING

Hat **Tipp 8** dir geholfen, den Text zu verstehen? ◯ ja ◯ teilweise ◯ nein

The days of Ollie's week

10a CHOOSE YOUR TASK audio 2/28

A **What is your favourite day of the week? Draw a picture and label it.**
B **Listen to Ollie's week in TB10b again and read along. Practise reading the story out loud.**
C **Choose one of the seven pictures in TB10 and write about it.**

10b

Choose three of the pictures in TB10 and talk about them. Make notes first. Record yourself and edit your recording.

What a day

11 CHOOSE YOUR LEVEL audio 2/31

Listen to Ollie in TB11a again.

I Complete the sentences.

1 ______________ is my favourite day. 2 My favourite food is ______________.

3 I'm in the ______________, digging holes. 4 I ______________ after the squirrels.

5 Ava doesn't ______________ with me. 6 She has a lot of ______________.

7 We don't ______________ any spaghetti. 8 What a ______________ Wednesday!

II Correct the sentences.

1 Ollie doesn't like Wednesdays. ______________

2 Ollie wants to eat spaghetti alone. ______________

3 Ava is happy when she comes home. ______________

4 She doesn't have to do any homework. ______________

5 Ava is very nice to Ollie. ______________

III Why is Ava's day so bad? What do you think? Write about it in your exercise book.

More sorting

12

Sort the words and phrases into the lists.

take out the rubbish · Saturday · walk in the park · ~~kitchen~~ ·
play a board game · Wednesday · bedroom · clean the bathroom

rooms in the house	chores	activities	days of the week
kitchen			

Challenge: Write more words or phrases in each list.

A typical week TARGET TASK SUPPORT

13 wordbank: time p. 155, at home p. 158, free time p. 157, skill: presentations p. 146

1 Make notes about your week or someone else's week.

day of the week	chores	activities	how often?
Monday			
Tuesday			
Wednesday			
Thursday			
Friday			
Saturday			
Sunday			

2 Complete the sentences. Choose the sentences you want to use.

My week

On Mondays, I usually come home from school at ______ o'clock. In the afternoon I go to ______________________.

She helps me with my ______________ homework. On Tuesdays, I always help my mum with ______________.

On Wednesdays, my friends and I often meet in ____________________________. We play __________________

or just relax. On Thursdays, I often go to ________________________ and we play ________________________.

On Fridays, my mum and I sometimes go into town and ______________________. On Saturdays, I usually do

nothing. On Sundays, my family and I ____. And sometimes

we ____.

Tipp: Eine gute Collage erstellen

1 Für eine Collage brauchst du vor allem einen großen Bogen Papier. Außerdem benötigst du eine Schere, Kleber, einen Bleistift, bunte Stifte.

2 Mache dir zuerst mit Bleistift Notizen auf einem DIN A4 Blatt. Zeichne ein, wo du Bilder und Texte aufkleben möchtest, wo die Überschriften stehen sollen und wie viel Platz du für eigene Texte oder Illustrationen hast, die du zeichnen möchtest.

3 Erst wenn du mit der Aufteilung zufrieden bist, beginne die Collage auf deinem großen Blatt. Markiere zuerst wieder alles mit Bleistift. Wenn du sicher bist, dass alles gut aufgeteilt ist, kannst du mit farbigen Stiften arbeiten und deine Bilder aufkleben.

Die Check out-Seiten helfen dir einzuschätzen, was du schon gut kannst und was du noch üben solltest. Löse die Aufgaben auf dieser Doppelseite und male die Kreise wie auf Seite 28 rot, gelb oder grün aus.

1 Kannst du in einem Gespräch Vorschläge machen?
2 Kannst du Fragen mit Fragewort stellen?
3 Kannst du sagen, wem etwas gehört?
4 Kannst du kurze Textnachrichten verstehen?
5 Kannst du verstehen, wenn jemand von seiner Woche berichtet?
6 Kannst du sagen, was jemand wie häufig macht?

1

How do you say this in English? Write it down.

1 Du willst deinen Freunden vorschlagen, dass ihr in den Park gehen könnt. Was sagst du?

____

2 Du möchtest sagen: Lasst uns Videospiele spielen. Wie formulierst du das?

____

3 Was sagst du, wenn du eine Idee hast?

____

4 Wie drückst du aus, wenn du dir nicht sicher bist?

____

5 Wie kannst du einen Vorschlag loben?

____

Ich kann in einem Gespräch Vorschläge machen. ○

2

Complete the questions with question words.

1 ______ do you like to do after school?
2 ______ does Ava have breakfast?
3 ______ old is your cat?
4 ______ is my English folder? I can't find it.
5 ______ is Lily's best friend?
6 ______ many pencils have you got?

Ich kann Fragen mit Fragewort stellen. ○

3

Fill in the right names. Use s-genitives.

Ava · Ava's family · Harry · Harry and Lily · Mr Hu · Tarek

1 Lily is ______ sister.
2 Noah and Joshua are ______ brothers.
3 Double and Trouble are ______ pets.
4 Sami is ______ uncle.
5 The children buy snacks at ______ corner shop.
6 Ollie is ______ dog.

Ich kann sagen, wem etwas gehört. ○

4

Read the text messages and tick ✓ yes or no.

Lily
We need rabbit food. Can you buy some? Fri, 6:10pm

Harry
Why can't you do it? ☹ You know that I'm at Tarek's place. We want to watch a film now. Fri, 6:13pm

Lily
OK, OK. I don't always know about all your plans. I can go to the pet shop. Fri, 6:17pm

Harry
Good. And can you go to Mr Hu's corner shop on the way and get some biscuits for me? Fri, 6:20pm

Lily
Oh, sure. I love to go shopping for you. Anything else I can do for you? Fri, 6:22pm

		yes	no
1	Does Harry want to buy rabbit food?	☐	☐
2	Does he want to come home soon?	☐	☐
3	Do Harry and Tarek want to play video games?	☐	☐
4	Does Lily want to go to the pet shop and the corner shop?	☐	☐

Ich kann kurze Textnachrichten verstehen. ◯

5 audio 2/32

Listen to Jacinda talking about her week and match the sentence parts.

1 On Mondays
2 On Tuesday and Thursdays
3 On Fridays
4 On Saturdays
5 On Sundays

Jacinda and her mum clean the house.
Jacinda meets her dad.
they meet Jacinda's grandma or go to the park.
Jacinda goes to the science club.
it's her turn to make dinner.

Ich kann verstehen, wenn jemand von seiner Woche berichtet. ◯

6

Unscramble the sentences.

1 makes breakfast · Noah · on Sundays · never ____________________

2 dinner · sometimes · he · cleans up · after ____________________

3 takes Ollie for a walk · often · feeds him · and · he

____

4 for his grandma · does the shopping · Noah · on Fridays · always

____

Ich kann sagen, was jemand wie häufig macht. ◯

Wenn du noch mehr üben möchtest, gehe zu Practise more - Unit 4. DIGITAL+

The best birthday

1a

Collect birthday words in the word web.
When you think about birthdays, what can you
- **smell?**
- **see?**
- **taste?**
- **feel?**
- **hear?**

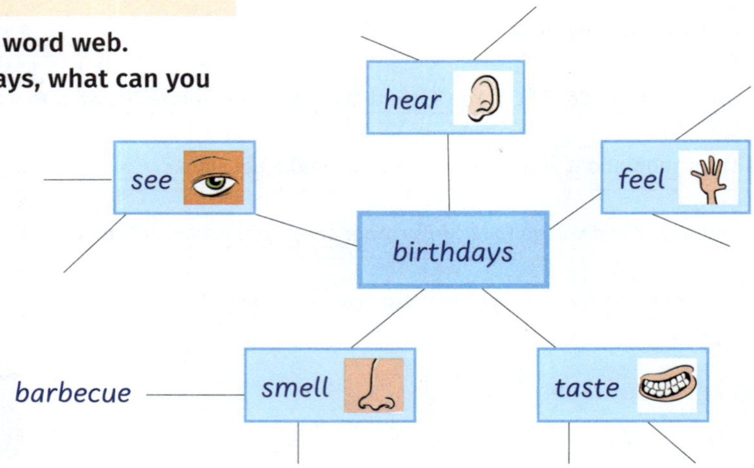

1b video 16

Watch the video clip in TB1b again. Tick ✓ the correct answers.

1 How many birthday presents does Maxine like?
- ☐ just one
- ☐ lots
- ☐ two

2 What kind of birthday cake does Emily like?
- ☐ chocolate
- ☐ lemon
- ☐ strawberry

3 Where does Ben like to have his birthday party?
- ☐ in the pool with music
- ☐ in the garden with his family
- ☐ in the garden with his friends

4 Why does her dad make pancakes for Hannah?
- ☐ because they are very special pancakes
- ☐ because they are Hannah's favourite breakfast
- ☐ because only he can make them

1c

Do a survey about birthdays in your class. Walk around and ask classmates what they like about birthdays.

name	activities	food and drink	other things

1d

Tell the class about the survey.
You can say:
Elmar likes birthdays with all his friends.
Nino loves to have a picnic in the park.
The best birthday for Elfie is when she makes pizza with her family.

Ava's birthday plans

2a audio 2/33

Listen to Ava and her parents in TB2a again. How many people does Ava invite to the party?

________ people

2b CHOOSE YOUR LEVEL

I Listen again. Match the notes.

Ava's birthday	pizza in the garden
Ava's guests	garden party, barbecue and pool
what Ava wants to do first	4th June
what dad says	garden party, barbecue, pool and selfie box
Mum's ideas for the party	friends and family
what they are planning in the end	go bowling

II Listen again. Tick ✓ the correct answers.

1 Ava's birthday
- ☐ 12th May
- ☐ 4th June
- ☐ 12th June

2 Ava's guests
- ☐ only friends
- ☐ friends and family
- ☐ Grandma Edyta

3 What Ava wants to do for her birthday
- ☐ have a barbecue
- ☐ go bowling
- ☐ eat pizza

4 Dad's idea for the party
- ☐ pizza in the garden
- ☐ go swimming
- ☐ a funny clown

5 Mum's ideas for the party
- ☐ go to Poland
- ☐ go bowling
- ☐ garden party with barbecue

6 What they are planning in the end
- ☐ garden party, barbecue, pool, selfie box
- ☐ garden party with pizza
- ☐ garden party with a funny clown

III Listen again. Take notes.

1 When is Ava's birthday? ________

2 Who can Ava not invite? ________

3 How many of the guests are children? ________

4 What does Ava want to do? ________

5 What is her dad's idea? ________

6 What is her mum's idea? ________

7 What are they planning in the end? ________

Ava's garden party

3a

Read TB3a again. Tick ✓ true or false.

	true	false
1 Joshua is writing invitations.	☐	☐
2 Noah and Ava are making a mess.	☐	☐
3 Noah is buying some more food.	☐	☐
4 The guests are bringing presents.	☐	☐
5 Ava is opening her presents.	☐	☐
6 Joshua is jumping into the pool.	☐	☐

Challenge: Correct the false sentences in your exercise book.

3b CHOOSE YOUR LEVEL

grammar: present progressive statements p. 181

Look at the pictures. What are the people doing? What aren't they doing?
I Write four sentences. II Write six sentences. III Write eight or more sentences.

Tarek and Ollie Joshua and Aunt Hannah Ollie ...	is isn't are aren't	wearing decorating taking kissing ...	a birthday song. grandma. party hats. a selfie. the garden. ...

1 *Tarek and Ollie are wearing* ______________________

2 ______________________

3 ______________________

4 ______________________

5 ______________________

6 ______________________

7 ______________________

8 ______________________

LANGUAGE HELP — das Datum

Im Britischen Englisch gibt es zwei Schreibweisen für das Datum: Entweder *14 April* oder *14th April*.
Wenn man es ausspricht, sagt man: *the fourteenth of April*.
Für *1 May* oder *1st May* sagt man *the first of May*, für *2 June* oder *2nd June* sagt man *the second of June*.

The months of the year

4a wordbank: time p. 155

Find the months in the word snake.

NOVEMBER|MARCHSEPTEMBERFEBRUARYJULYMAY

DECEMBEROCTOBERJANUARYJUNEAPRILAUGUST

4b

Answer the questions.

1 Which month comes before March? ______

2 Which month has only three letters? ______

3 Which two months start with the letter M? ______

4 Which three months are in winter? ______

Challenge: Write two more questions for a partner. ______

______

4c audio 2/35

Listen to the children. Tick ✓ the correct answers.

1 Noah's birthday
- ☐ 22nd May
- ☐ 23rd March
- ☐ 22nd March

2 Lily and Ollie's birthday
- ☐ 4th December
- ☐ 14th December
- ☐ 14th October

3 Tarek's birthday
- ☐ 21st July
- ☐ 23rd July
- ☐ 23rd June

4d wordbank: time p. 155

When is everyone's birthday? Write down the dates.

1 My birthday is on the twenty-first day of the year.

______

2 My birthday is on the last day of the year.

______

3 My birthday is on the first day of the eighth month.

______

4 My birthday is on the fourth day of the sixth month.

______

5 My birthday is on the fifteenth day of the eleventh month.

______

6 My birthday is on the second day of the fifth month.

______

All the family

5a

Find twelve family words in the grid. Write them down.

→ ← ↓ ↑

V	R	E	H	T	O	M	D	N	A	R	G
D	K	C	N	D	N	A	B	S	U	H	Z
A	Q	T	O	J	A	V	Q	U	M	I	S
U	B	U	S	I	S	T	E	R	K	B	Y
G	R	A	N	D	F	A	T	H	E	R	W
H	O	C	Z	V	I	U	T	U	D	E	J
T	T	Y	K	B	U	N	C	L	E	H	S
E	H	M	R	E	H	T	O	M	C	T	W
R	E	I	D	Q	U	Y	V	K	Z	A	M
M	R	S	K	J	T	A	U	W	I	F	E

5b wordbank: family p. 160

Complete the sentences about Ava's family.

1 Helen is Noah's ______

2 Daniel is Robert's ______

3 Mia and Daniel are Ava's ______

4 Sebastian is Fiona's ______

5 Mark is Hannah's ______

6 Fiona is Mia's ______

An invitation

6 CHOOSE YOUR TASK wordbank: party time p. 161

A **Ava is writing invitations. Fill in the information.**

B **Make a dictionary with words for family members in English and German or another language you know. Draw pictures, too.**

C **Make a meal plan for a themed party.**

Dear ______

Please come to ______

on ______ *at* ______ *o'clock*

Our plans: ______

______

Please bring: ______

Sound check

7a audio 2/36

Learn to say the letters 'v' and 'w'.
Listen to the words and repeat them.

van · welcome · window · visit · wash · very · week · vanilla · winter · verb · website · video · vegetarian

7b

Find more words that start with 'v' or 'w'. Write them down and practise saying them.

Practise reading

Tipp 9
Es kann dir helfen, Informationen im Text zu unterstreichen oder zu markieren und sie beispielsweise in einer Tabelle, einem Diagramm oder einem Wortnetz *(word web)* zu sortieren.

Tarek's birthday party

8a audio 2/37

Read the text. Underline what you find out about the party idea.

An alien themed party
Dress up as aliens, astronauts and planets and have an "aliens and space" party!

What you need	First, you need a great costume. To look like something out of this world, create your own costume, for example a space suit with a funny helmet. Or paint your face to look like an alien!
Activities	You can do karaoke to songs about the sun, the moon, the stars and the planets.
Food	You can eat astronaut ice cream! Astronauts eat this kind of ice cream in space and you can buy it in special shops.
Decorations	You can put up small lights that look like stars and use glitter.

8b

Make a word web with the information from the text.

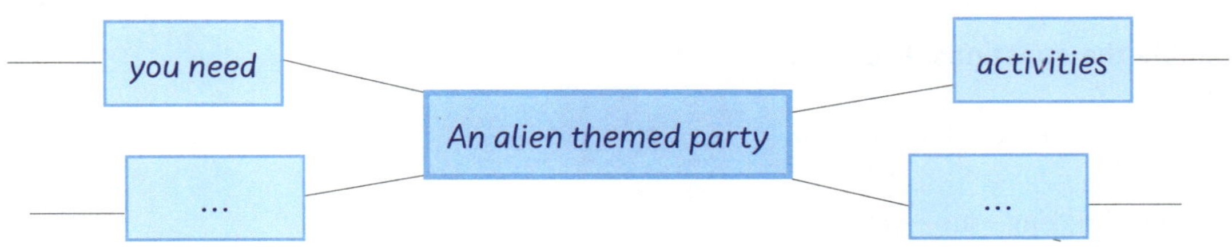

PRACTISE READING

Hat **Tipp 9** dir geholfen, den Text zu verstehen? ◯ ja ◯ teilweise ◯ nein

Party tips

9 audio 2/38

Listen to the party tip podcast. Tick ✓ the correct answers.

1. Der Podcast ist eine Anleitung, um ☐ Partyhüte zu machen. ☐ Partycracker zu machen.
2. Man braucht dafür ☐ leere Toilettenpapierrollen. ☐ kleine Kästchen.
3. Man kann sie füllen mit ☐ kleinen lustigen Dingen. ☐ buntem Papier.
4. Mehr Informationen gibt es ☐ im Radio. ☐ auf der Webseite.

Happy birthday, Tarek!

10a CHOOSE YOUR LEVEL audio 2/39

Listen to TB12a again.

I Match the questions and the answers.

1 Is Uncle Sami calling Tarek on the phone?	Yes, they are.
2 Are the children eating astronaut ice cream?	No, she isn't.
3 Is Ava wearing a space cowboy costume?	No, it isn't.
4 Is the space treasure hunt in the kitchen?	Yes, he is.

II Unscramble the questions. Then match the questions and the answers.

1 Tarek's uncle – singing – Is – a birthday song? ______	No, he isn't.
2 the children – eating? – are – What ______	No, he isn't.
3 space suit? – Is – wearing – Tarek – a ______	Crisps and astronaut ice cream.
4 Is – the living room – cleaning – Tarek's dad? ______	Yes, he is.

III Unscramble the questions. Then answer them.

1 Tarek's – singing – is – what – uncle ______

2 the children – drinking – are – what ______

3 move – his hands – Harry – can't – why ______

4 the treasure hunt – is – on the – moon ______

10b audio 2/40

Listen to the English words and repeat them. Match them to the German words.

astronaut ice cream · space suit · robot-alien · treasure hunt · moon stones

außerirdischer Roboter · Mondsteine · Astronauteneiscreme · Raumanzug · Schatzsuche

10c grammar: present progressive statements p.181

Look at the picture of the party and take notes. What is happening? What is not happening? Talk about the picture and record yourself. Edit your recording.

Planning a cool birthday party TARGET TASK SUPPORT

11 wordbank: party time p. 161, skill: presentations p. 146

1 Collect ideas for a cool birthday party.

Place: ______ Activities: ______

Guests: ______ Food and drink: ______

Music: ______ Decorations: ______

2 Write your lists.

GUEST LIST

GAMES

PLAYLIST

TO-DO LIST

SHOPPING LIST

Tipp: Eine digitale Collage erstellen

1 Für eine digitale Collage brauchst du weder Papier noch Schere oder Klebstoff. Alles, was du zum Thema zeigen möchtest, erstellst du digital und sammelst es in einem Odner auf deinem Laptop oder Computer.

2 Bei der Planung deiner Geburstagsparty kannst du Listen erstellen, Texte schreiben, eine bunte Einladungskarte entwerfen und Fotos sammeln.

3 Wenn du Gegenstände zeigen möchtest, fotografiere sie und stelle die Fotos in deinen Ordner.

4 Bei der Präsentation erklärst du mithilfe deiner digitalen Collage, welche Party du geplant hast und was alles dazugehört.

A day out in Brighton

1a audio 2/42

Listen to the words and repeat them. Find the words in the text in TB1b.

scared · seagull · beach · fatbike · Brighton · crazy · weren't · day trip · photos · pier

1b

Look at the picture of Brighton. Tick ✓ the caption you like best.

☐ At the beach

☐ A sunny day in Brighton

☐ Cool skaters in Brighton

Challenge: **Say why you think it is the best caption.**

Last year in Brighton

2 CHOOSE YOUR LEVEL grammar: simple past of be p. 183

Match the sentence parts.

1 That was	scared of the seagull?
2 It was	we were.
3 Weren't you	very hungry!
4 Oh yes,	a really crazy seagull.

Unscramble the sentences.

1 pier. · at · was · This · the
2 that · at Brighton · Was · too? · beach,
3 was · seagull. · That · crazy · a really
4 seagull? · you · of · scared · Weren't · the

1 ______
2 ______
3 ______
4 ______

Unscramble the sentences.

1 my · time · was · first · It
2 very · Harry · at · good · it · wasn't
3 seagull · That · really · was · crazy · a
4 scared · Weren't · the · of · you · seagull
5 at · Brighton · Was · that · too · beach,
6 were · Harry and I · there · friends · some · with

1 ______
2 ______
3 ______
4 ______
5 ______
6 ______

What about the weather?

3 CHOOSE YOUR LEVEL

sunny · warm · windy[1] · rainy · hot · cold · foggy[2] · cloudy[3] · nice · wet

1 **windy** – windig, 2 **foggy** – neblig, 3 **cloudy** – wolkig

I **Write weather words under the picture. Circle your favourite day.**

II **Write about the weather.**

On Friday the weather is ______

On Saturday ______

On Sunday ______

I like the weather on ______ because ______

III **Write about the weather on each day in your exercise book. Which day do you like best? Why?**

Challenge: **What is the weather like where you are? Write about it in your exercise book.**
Today the weather is … in …

Going to Brighton

4a audio 2/43

Listen to Harry and his mum in TB2a again. Write down: who is coming to Brighton?

______

4b

Are the sentences true or false? Tick ✓ .

	true	false
1 Lily and Harry want to show Noah the beach in Brighton.	☐	☐
2 Brighton is not too far from London.	☐	☐
3 Harry and his mum check the weather.	☐	☐
4 They want to go on Sunday.	☐	☐
5 They book tickets for the train at 10 o'clock.	☐	☐
6 Ava's mum is coming, too.	☐	☐

Challenge: Correct the false sentences in your exercise book.

A day in Brighton

5 CHOOSE YOUR LEVEL grammar: simple past of be p. 183

I Complete the sentences with the words in the box.

weren't · was (4x) · were · wasn't

1 Today ________ an exciting day! 2 I ________ at the beach but there ________ any people there. 3 So there ________ no food around. 4 Then there ________ some children on the beach with a yummy sandwich. 5 And swoosh! – I ________ hungry anymore. 6 I ________ a happy seagull with a yummy sandwich!

II Write six sentences about a day in Brighton.

We It There Some of the tricks My friend and I It	was were	really hard. some cool fatbikes for us. very good at it. so much fun! great! at Brighton beach today.

III Write a diary entry about a day in Brighton in your exercise book.

Who was with you? How was the weather?
How was the food? What was the best thing about the day?

You can write:

<u>My day in Brighton</u>
I was at …

They weren't in Brighton

6 grammar: simple past of be p. 183

Where were they? Where weren't they? Write sentences.

1 Harry ~~bike park~~ beach
2 Lily ~~kitchen~~ lab
3 Ava ~~school~~ home
4 Double and Trouble ~~cage~~ garden
5 Tarek ~~gym~~ cafeteria
6 Mr Hu ~~shop~~ park

1 Harry wasn't at the bike park, he was at the beach.

The video message

7a video 18

Watch the video clip in TB5b again. Number the sights in the correct order.

☐ the Lanes
☐ Brighton Palace Pier
☐ i360 tower
☐ Royal Pavilion
☐ Upside Down House

7b

Write down your top 3 sights.

Challenge: Answer the questions.

1 What can you see or do at the pier?
2 What is special about the Upside Down House?
3 How old is the Royal Pavilion?
4 What can you buy at the souvenir shop?
5 What are the Lanes?

Noah's message to his friends

8 CHOOSE YOUR LEVEL

I Unscramble the words and complete the sentences.

Hi guys, thanks for the great ______________ (i-d-e-v-o)! I really like the amusement park on the ______________ (r-i-e-p). The i360 ______________ (w-r-t-e-o) is so cool – weren't you scared? Please, don't bring me a seagull T-shirt as a ______________ (v-u-s-e-r-i-n-o)! Have fun! Noah

II Number the sentences in a good order.

☐ Now I really want to go to Brighton, too!
☐ The i360 and the Royal Pavilion are my favourite things.
☐ See you soon, Noah.
☐ Hi guys, what a cool video!
☐ Can you please bring me a Brighton Rock candy stick as a souvenir?

III Write Noah's message in your exercise book.

Say thank you for the video.
Say what you like about it. (two things)
Ask for something special as a souvenir.
Say goodbye at the end of the message.

Rules at the pier

9

Look at the rules. What do they mean? Take notes in German.

1

2

3

4

5

____

____

____

Seaside towns

10 CHOOSE YOUR TASK

A **Draw a postcard of Brighton and label it.**
B **Create a word search with Brighton words.**
C **Find out about food you can eat in British seaside towns. Tell the class about it.**

Practise reading

Tipp 10
Unterstreiche im Text alle Wörter, die du kennst. Manchmal erkennst du noch mehr Wörter, wenn du dir den Text anhörst. Unbekannte Wörter, die dir wichtig erscheinen, solltest du im Wörterbuch nachschlagen.

Shopping in Brighton

11a

Read the two dialogues. Underline all the words you know.

Ava: Excuse me. I'm looking for a postcard of Brighton Pier.
Shopkeeper: The postcards are over there, next to the comic books.
Ava: Oh thanks. – I'd like this one, please.
Shopkeeper: That's 95p, please. Would you like a stamp, too?
Ava: Oh yes! One for a postcard to Poland, please. How much is it then?
Shopkeeper: That's 1 pound 80, please.
Ava: Here you are.
Shopkeeper: And 3 pounds 20 change.
Ava: Thank you. Have a nice day.
Shopkeeper: Thanks, you too. Bye.

Shopkeeper: Hi, can I help you?
Harry: Yes, please. Have you got this T-shirt in red?
Shopkeeper: Just a minute. Let me have a look ... Here is one. What size do you need?
Harry: Size M, please.
Shopkeeper: Here you are.
Harry: Oh great. I think it fits. How much is it?
Shopkeeper: It's 15 pounds 99.
Harry: Cool. I'll take it. Where can I pay?
Shopkeeper: The till is over there.
Harry: Thanks for your help. Bye.
Shopkeeper: No problem. Bye.

11b audio 2/48

Listen to the dialogues and read along. Can you underline more words now?

11c

Write down the words you don't know. Look up the words you think are important.

PRACTISE READING

Hat **Tipp 10** dir geholfen, den Text zu verstehen? ◯ ja ◯ teilweise ◯ nein

Mum's day out

12a

Look at the pictures. Number the sentences in a good order.

1

2

3

☐ Then we had tea in the garden.
☐ We were at the beach.
☐ I like Mulan a lot.

[1] I was at my friend Mulan's house.
☐ It was so nice to see her again.
☐ She has a new baby, Liu.

☐ He is so cute.
☐ It was sunny and warm there.

12b

grammar: simple past of be p. 183

Look at the pictures. Answer the questions. Choose short answers from the box.

1

2

3

4

5

6

7

8

Yes, they were. · Yes, she was. · No, she wasn't. · No, she wasn't. · No, they weren't. · Yes, he was. · Yes, they were. · No, he wasn't.

1 Was Lily at Mulan's house? ______
2 Were Sarah and Mulan at the beach? ______
3 Were Lily and Harry in Mulan's garden? ______
4 Was Sarah at Brighton Pier? ______
5 Was Tarek on the i360 tower? ______
6 Were Sarah and Mulan at the Upside Down House? ______
7 Was Liu at the Royal Pavilion? ______
8 Was Ava at the souvenir shop? ______

Writing a postcard
TARGET TASK SUPPORT

13 wordbank: places p. 152, free time p. 157, food p. 156, skill: writing p 143

1 Who do you want to write to? Collect ideas.

____

2 Complete the text and tick ✓ the ideas you like. Choose the sentences you want to use.

☐ Dear Grandma Rosie,	☐ Hi ________,	☐ Hello Uncle Agba,
☐ I'm on a day out in Hamburg.	☐ I'm on holiday in Ibiza.	☐ I'm in ________ for the weekend.
☐ I'm here with my family.	☐ I'm here with my friends.	☐ I'm here with ________.
☐ First I was at the swimming pool.	☐ After breakfast, we were at the beach.	☐ In the morning, we ________.
☐ Then we had lunch.	☐ In the afternoon, we looked at the seagulls.	☐ Before dinner, we were ________.

☐ My favourite activity was ______________________________.

☐ It was lots of fun!	☐ We had a great time!	☐ It was very boring!
☐ The food was OK!	☐ The food was ________.	☐ The food was not my thing.
☐ The weather was sunny.	☐ The weather was rainy.	☐ The weather was ________.
☐ I love it here!	☐ I wish you were here!	☐ I can't wait to come home!
☐ Love, ________	☐ All the best, ________	☐ See you soon, ________

3 Now write your postcard in your exercise book.

- Say hello.
- Say where you are.
- Say who is with you.
- Say how you like it there.
- What was the best thing?
- What was your favourite food?
- What was the weather like?
- Say goodbye.

Tipp: Eine Postkarte schreiben

1 Kaufe zunächst eine schöne Ansichtskarte, auf der man sieht, wo du bist.
2 Dann kannst du etwas über das Bild darauf erzählen und deine eigenen Eindrücke dazu schildern.
3 Sage, wie es dir geht. Erzähle, was du erlebt hast und was dir besonders gut gefallen hat.
4 Auf einer Postkarte ist nicht viel Platz. Überlege daher vorher, was du sagen willst.
5 Ganz wichtig: Schreibe so ordentlich, dass man deine Karte auch lesen kann.

Die Check out-Seiten helfen dir einzuschätzen, was du schon gut kannst und was du noch üben solltest. Löse die Aufgaben auf dieser Doppelseite und male die Kreise wie auf Seite 28 rot, gelb oder grün aus.

1. Kannst du beschreiben, was jemand gerade tut?
2. Kennst du Wörter, um über Familienmitglieder und deren Geburtstage zu sprechen?
3. Kannst du Tipps für eine besondere Geburtstagsfeier verstehen?
4. Kannst du sagen, wo jemand in der Vergangenheit war oder nicht war?
5. Kannst du den Inhalt einer Durchsage verstehen und das Wichtigste auf Deutsch wiedergeben?
6. Kannst du einen Einkaufsdialog führen?

1 grammar: present progressive statements TB p. 181

It's Sunday morning. Write down what everybody is doing.

Joshua – listen to music · Noah – brush his teeth · Ava – lie on her bed · Mr Kogan – do yoga · Mrs Kogan – read a book · Ollie – play with his ball

Ich kann beschreiben, was jemand gerade tut. ◯

2

Look at the family tree and talk about it.
Talk about the birthdays, too.
Say six or more sentences.
Make a recording.

mother · father · daughter · son · sister · brother · cousin · aunt · uncle · wife · husband

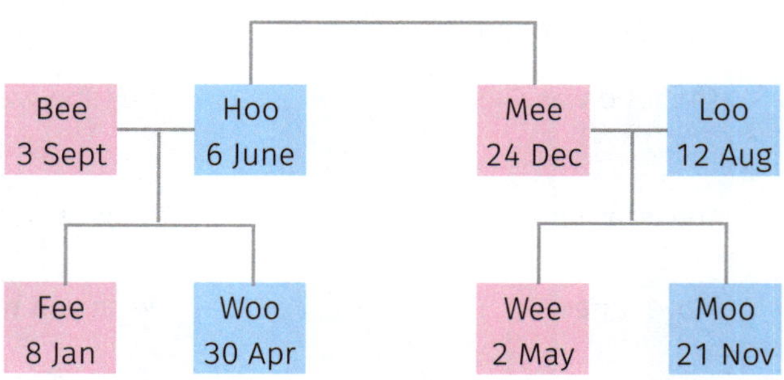

Ich kenne Wörter, um über Familienmitglieder und deren Geburtstage zu sprechen. ◯

3

Read the tips for a special birthday party. Then answer the questions in German in your exercise book.

An outdoor film night

Watch great films in your garden or behind your house.
It is the perfect idea for summer birthdays!

What you need: one or two good films, a computer and a screen, chairs or mattresses
Food and drinks: water and lemonade
lots of popcorn and snacks
Tips: Design cinema tickets for your guests.
Ask them to dress up as their favourite film character.

1. Wo kann eine Filmnacht im Freien stattfinden?
2. Für wen ist das eine gute Idee?
3. Was braucht man dafür?
4. Um was kann man die Gäste bitten?

Ich kann Tipps für eine besondere Geburtstagsfeier verstehen. ◯

4

Where were the people yesterday afternoon? Where weren't they? Write about them.

1 Tarek: ~~at the park~~ at the ice rink

2 Lily: ~~at Ava's place~~ at Portobello Road Market with her mums

3 Harry: ~~in town with his friends~~ at school with the school band

4 Joshua: ~~at home~~ at the playground with his dad

Ich kann sagen, wo jemand in der Vergangenheit war oder nicht war.

5 audio 2/50

Listen to the announcement on a train. Answer the questions in German.

1 Wann kommt der Zug in London an?

2 Wo sollen die Passagiere aussteigen?

3 Was sollen die Passagiere noch beachten?

Ich kann den Inhalt einer Durchsage verstehen und das Wichtigste auf Deutsch wiedergeben.

6

Work with a partner. Act out the dialogue. Make a recording.

Partner / Partnerin A
Du arbeitest in einem Laden an der Ecke.

1 Begrüße B und frage, ob du helfen kannst.
3 Bejahe und sage, dass sie im Kühlschrank neben dem Käse sind.
5 Sage: „Natürlich, hier bitte." Sage dann, dass es 6 Pfund 50 kostet.
7 Sage, wie viel Wechselgeld B zurückbekommt.
9 Bedanke dich und wünsche B auch einen schönen Tag. Verabschiede dich dann.

Partner / Partnerin B
Du gehst als Kunde / Kundin in den Laden an der Ecke.

2 Begrüße A und frage, ob er / sie vegetarische Würstchen hat.
4 Bedanke dich. Frage A dann, ob du auch Schokoladenplätzchen haben könntest.
6 Sage: „Hier bitte – 10 Pfund."
8 Bedanke dich und wünsche A einen schönen Tag.

Ich kann einen Einkaufsdialog führen.

Wenn du noch mehr üben möchtest, gehe zu Practise more - Unit 5. DIGITAL+

Welche der 10 Tipps fandest du in diesem Schuljahr hilfreich? Merke sie dir besonders gut.

Tipp 1 – Unit 1A

Bevor du einen Text liest, sieh dir die Überschrift an und überlege, worum es gehen könnte.

Tipp 2 – Unit 1B

Es gibt viele Wörter, die im Englischen und im Deutschen ähnlich oder sogar gleich sind. Es kann helfen, nach solchen Wörtern zu schauen, wenn du einen Text liest.

Tipp 3 – Unit 2A

Wenn es zu einem Text Bilder gibt, sieh sie dir an. Sie können dir Hinweise auf den Inhalt des Textes geben.

Tipp 4 – Unit 2B

Wenn du genaue Informationen aus einem Text herauslesen willst, kannst du ihn nach und nach durchgehen. Folgende Fragen können dir helfen:

What? (Was?) Who? (Wer?) When? (Wann?) Where? (Wo?)

Tipp 5 – Unit 3A

Es kann dir helfen, während des Lesens einen Text durch Unterstreichungen oder Markierungen zu strukturieren.

Tipp 6 – Unit 3B

Versuche, die Wörter, die du beim Lesen nicht gleich verstehst, aus dem Textzusammenhang oder aus der Situation zu erschließen. Nutze dabei dein Allgemeinwissen.

Tipp 7 – Unit 4A

Denke nach, bevor du liest! Es hilft dir oft, wenn du überlegst, was du schon über ein Thema weißt, bevor du einen Text darüber liest.

Tipp 8 – Unit 4B

Überfliege einen langen Text zuerst. Schaue dir die Zwischenüberschriften und Bilder an. Dann suche im Text gezielt nach Wörtern, die zu den Bildern passen *(scan the text)*. Lies dabei nicht jedes Wort.

Tipp 9 – Unit 5A

Es kann dir helfen, Informationen im Text zu unterstreichen oder zu markieren und sie beispielsweise in einer Tabelle, einem Diagramm oder einem Wortnetz *(word web)* zu sortieren.

Tipp 10 – Unit 5B

Unterstreiche im Text alle Wörter, die du kennst. Manchmal erkennst du noch mehr Wörter, wenn du dir den Text anhörst. Unbekannte Wörter, die dir wichtig erscheinen, solltest du im Wörterbuch nachschlagen.

Bildquellen

|Alamy Stock Photo (RMB), Abingdon/Oxfordshire: Sherratt, Adrian 57.7; © Tetra Images 7.2. |Eckardt, Jasmin, Wiesbaden: 59.1. |fotolia.com, New York: dudadidi 57.9; pete pahham 57.8. |Imago, Berlin: Schmidt, Norbert 57.6. |iStockphoto.com, Calgary: 7stock 57.1; Bikeworldtravel 20.1; Daniela Buoncristiani 7.1; master1305 57.3; Moussa81 Titel; Natissima 57.4; Westend 61 7.3. |juniors@wildlife Bildagentur GmbH, Hamburg: Wegler, M. 16.1. |Koerner, Amy, Frankfurt am Main: 18.1. |Minkus Images Fotodesignagentur, Isernhagen: 57.5. |Picture-Alliance GmbH, Frankfurt a.M.: dpa 18.2; imageBROKER 9.1; ZB/M. Hiekel 57.2. |Shutterstock.com, New York: agsaz 99.1; Nolte, Lourens 47.1; zhengzaishuru 10.1. |stock.adobe.com, Dublin: Kneschke, Robert 64.1; mimagephotos 7.4.

Videoclips

2 That's me!
8 This is our school
11 What's their sport?
14 This is my room
16 Birthday fun
18 A message from Brighton

Namen der Sprecher und Sprecherinnen der Videoclips und Audiotracks

Brian Bowles, Jaden Christopher, India Dowers, Naomi Frederick, Max Iverney, Isa Jones, Daphne Kouma, Samyar Mahrouyan, Gina Murray, Chris Nayak, Roisin Rankin, George Weightman

Über diesen QR-Code gelangst du auf die Webseite
www.westermann.de/128210
Dort findest du alle Audiotracks, Videoclips, Arbeitsblätter zur Medienbildung und die Practise more Arbeitsblätter.